Finding the Lost
UNIVERSAL PRINCIPLES

Finding the Lost
UNIVERSAL PRINCIPLES
The Three Little Pigs unlock the door

by

Patricia Pillard McCulley

Interdimensional Press
Brentwood, California 94513

© 2010 Patricia Pillard McCulley. All Rights Reserved.

No part of this book may be reproduced, stored in a retrieval system, or transmitted by any means without the written permission of the author.

Visit the website for information about the author and other resources.
www.FindingTheLostUniversalPrinciples.com

First published by Interdimentional Press, 06/2010

ISBN: 978-0-9827753-0-1

Library of Congress Control Number: 2010929012

Printed in the United States of America

Cover Design and Illustrations by E. Byron McCulley

DEDICATION

This book is dedicated to my loving husband, Byron, who has been extremely flexible with the immense changes in my life, and to my adult children, Wendy and Matthew, who I hope are no longer embarrassed by my "differentness."

TABLE OF CONTENTS

Acknowledgments……………………………………………..…………ix

Preface……………………………………………………………………xi

Introduction – The Three Little Pigs……………………………………1

Chapter 1 – Fairy Tale or Myth? ……………………………………….3

Chapter 2 – Question #1……………………………………………….5
    What can I reliably base my life on?

Chapter 3 -- Question #2………………………………………………21
    What do you do when evil gets in your house?

Chapter 4 -- How do we know what is true?……………..…………29

Chapter 5 – All Exists in Duality……………………………………….41

Chapter 6 – All is One…………………………………………………61
    All Physical is One………………………………………………63
    All People are One………………………………………………66
    Time and Space are One………………………………………75
    All Religions are One……………………………………………79

Chapter 7 – We are Spiritual Beings…………………………………91

Chapter 8 – The Unseen Controls the Seen………………………103

Chapter 9 -- Cause and Effect Always Occur Together………123

Chapter 10 – True Freedom is An Inner Attitude………………129

Chapter 11 -- Change is a Constant………………………………133

Chapter 12 -- After the Principles..139

Chapter 13 – 2012 and The Mayan Calendar......................143

Chapter 14 – Calling all Evolutionaries...............................153

Epilogue -- The Challenge to Love is Before Us......................165

Appendix A – List of Universal Principles..........................169

Appendix B – Letter to my son, 1986................................173

Appendix C – Letter to my son, 2009................................179

Endnotes...183

ACKNOWLEDGEMENTS

Thank you to The Creative Initiative Foundation, and especially Harry and Emilia Rathbun (in memoriam), who helped me with my earliest spiritual questions; to my Spirit Guides and my Master Spiritual Teachers; to my confidant and dear sounding board Carolyn Shaw-Teuber and our Gnostic study group, where I learned of Gnosticism, that we planned our lives to learn lessons to further perfect our souls.

Most likely this book would not have been written without the suggestion of Evanne Jordan and Ish. I am most thankful that I was led to have that psychic reading that day. I appreciate Alexis Summerfield and the Women of Light, where I experience richness in the Principles. Thank you to Marianna Sucher and Nina Brown who got me back on the spiritual path after my desert period; and to Sylvia Browne and the Novus Spiritus teachings which have made my life full of thankfulness, joy, understanding, and inner peace.

Thank you to Virginia Santini (in memoriam) who helped me understand my interdimensional nature through the works of Kryon and Lazaris. A special thanks to Lee Carroll, who channels Kryon, for offering the MP3 teachings free of charge on his website, www.kryon.com.

A big thank you to my husband, Byron, for the little pig illustrations, the book cover and helping with formatting. Sue Clark and her writing class have been invaluable, educating me in all aspects of writing. Thank you, Sue, for answering all my novice questions and looking over my chapters.

I give great thanks to my Spirit Guide, who during one of my meditations told me that they (a group) would probably not be able to grant my wish of any direct guidance for this book in time for publication, but gave me a present to help me. I saw a big box with a bow. When I undid the bow and took off the top of the box, I reached in and found a pair of eyeglasses. They had the clearest lenses I had ever seen. I touched the lenses because it looked like there was nothing there, but there was. This gift brought tears to my eyes, because I knew that we all view everything through a filter, like wearing glasses that hinder our perception. I tried to put on the new pair, but I found I had to take off my current pair (not literal) with the filtering lenses in order to put on the new ones. Thank you Guide for giving me these glasses, which enabled me to see more clearly to write this book.

I thank my beloved Himalayan cats, Sir Lancelot and Sir Pounce de Leon, and Persian cat, Lady Taffylena de Charmalot. They were with us too briefly and have crossed over the Rainbow Bridge. They gave me many lessons in detachment, surrender, faith, unconditional love, trust and being.

Thank you to all that I encounter in my life for enriching my journey and being my teachers.

Patricia Pillard McCulley
June 2010

PREFACE

Do you ever have questions about life, such as why doesn't it seem to make sense? Or have you ever wondered why things happen as they do? Do you ever ask what is life really about?

Perhaps life is like a game, but we don't know the rules and we don't know how to win. What if we are all playing the same game of life, but on different levels? Is the game we play competing with others, or only with ourselves? Is life to be considered as play, rather than the heavy drama it seems sometimes? What are the rules and how do we discover them?

In the 1960s, I began an active search for the answers to these questions, for the rules of the game. My search led me to two books by Raymond Moody, Jr., which made a major impact on my life: *Life After Life* and *Reflections on Life After Life*. In these books, the author had interviewed people who had near-death experiences. As these people were crossing over to the Other Side, many of them were asked by some Being, if they had learned to love. In addition, one was asked if he knew the Universal Principles. I had never heard those specific words before, and the words intrigued me. Were the Universal Principles the rules of the game of life? Did they hold the answers to my questions?

In those days, there were no computers and no Google search engines. I had to read books, attend seminars and evaluate my own experiences. I spent over 40 years compiling a list of what I considered to be Universal Principles.[1]

In 2007, I spoke with psychic counselor Evanne Jordan of Walnut Creek, California, about my interest in Universal Principles and the list I had developed. She said I should write a book. She saw me "walking on a road of diamonds." Her words excited me and scared me at the same time. I am not an experienced writer, except for those papers I begrudgingly wrote in college. In the next couple of hours, as I contemplated what she had said, I had a daydream and saw myself walking on that road. What was even more important, I saw myself picking up the diamonds and throwing them out into the universe. I felt obligated to the universe. I needed to write this book.

As you are reading, be aware of how your body is responding to each concept. You may get chills while reading something specific; it can be an indication your highest self has been touched. That concept is something you believe deeply within yourself.

It is with great joy that I share my deepest treasures with you. They are the principles and truths on which I base my life. They have given me the opportunity for great inner peace, freedom, joy, thankfulness and meaning. Hopefully, they will aid you on your journey as well, especially if you are new in seeking the rules of the game of life.

Blessings to you on your path,

Patricia Pillard McCulley
Brentwood, California
June 2010

INTRODUCTION

This book starts by highlighting the fairy tale, *The Three Little Pigs*. It first appeared in print in *Nursery Rhymes and Nursery Tales* in 1843,[1] but the story is thought to be much older. As with many fairy tales, retelling of the story over time changed it in many ways, and the deeper symbolic meanings have been lost. These symbolic meanings have nothing to do with what the pigs' houses were made of.

It is a simple children's story; yet it contains two powerful concepts that can lead to peace and understanding in your life. I don't know why I was so interested in that story in my youth; perhaps something in that book rang true to me on a deep level, more than a simple story would show. I somehow knew it was one of the keys in my path to understanding what life was all about.

As you probably remember, the three little pigs are trying to protect themselves from the "big, bad wolf," who is attempting to blow their houses down and eat them. I remember the story and see the pictures in the book as if I had it in front of me today, even though it was more than 60 years ago that I first read it. I distinctly remember what has been lost in recent versions -- what the interior of the pigs' houses were like, and what happened to the wolf. I have yet to find a copy of the book with the exact version of the story as I remember it, but I have found different versions that show parts of it.

One of the main differences in the older version I read is the pictures on the wall, inside each of the pigs' houses, which I took to mean was what the pig valued. I have included illustrations that resemble those pictures as I remember them. The other important difference is about what happened to the wolf. In modern versions, he runs away. In the original, he came down the chimney of the last house, ended up in a pot of boiling water, and the three pigs ate him. Why the change? Was it because some people saw the boiling and eating as an issue of cruelty to animals?

My husband and I read fairy tales to our children as they grew up and talked about the deeper meaning in the tales. We had studied myths and dream interpretation, so we were accustomed to looking at stories in a symbolic way. Perhaps that could be part of the reason I looked at the pig story in that light.

After being exposed to the concept of Universal Principles, I concluded that the simple English fairy tale contained two powerful principles. These two have offered me guidance, understanding and peace of mind in the most challenging times of my life, and I present them here. It was the start of my learning the rules of life, and answers to my earlier questions about life and the world. These principles have guided and molded my entire life.

FAIRY TALE OR MYTH?

The story *The Three Little Pigs* is a children's fairy tale, but also could be considered as having mythical characteristics. Joseph Campbell in his book, *Myths To Live By*, defines myth as a story that always is, but never was -- always true, but it never really happened. Wikipedia, The Free Encyclopedia, defines myth as the following:

> ...sacred narrative in the sense that it holds religious or spiritual significance for those who tell it, and it contributes to and expresses systems of thought and values. Use of the term by scholars implies neither the truth nor the falseness of the narrative. To the source culture, however, a myth by definition is "true," in that it embodies beliefs, concepts, and ways of questioning and making sense of the world.

Wikipedia states further:

> Myths are symbolic stories, and have a deeper meaning than what appears on the surface.

They can be considered to contain Universal Principles, which also may be called Spiritual Truths, in that they express values. (The Three Little Pigs could be termed one of the) 'how to live' myths, (which) will have a certain message portrayed through the story, and were created to teach us "how to live."

The pigs, the houses, the pictures on the inside walls, and the wolf all have meanings beyond the literal. Contrary to popular thought, the essence of the story has little to do with what the houses were made of.

PRINCIPLE #1:

WHAT CAN WE RELIABLY BASE OUR LIVES ON?

The Three Little Pigs tells us what happens if we base our life on illusion. If we don't build a strong house on a stable foundation, the wolf is likely to blow it down or get in some other way. The message comes to us in a symbolic way for the houses represent one's self.

How do you build a strong house, a strong foundation, and a strong self? What is true security in life? In the version of the book I remember reading as a five year old, the story conveys this by the pictures on the walls inside each of the pigs' houses. They show what is not secure, because in each case the wolf was able to get in.

The Physical

The picture on the wall of the first pig's house shows him as a body builder. He stood on his hind feet with a big ribbon across his chest stating, THE WINNER. His bulging muscles showed he most valued the physical and based his life on it. Can you count on, or base your life on your physical body? Anyone who has had any kind of physical problem or who has lived beyond the age of 50 can see the error in that scenario.

People who have been physical all their lives, especially if they have played in a professional sport and have relied on their physical prowess, often have a hard lesson to learn when their body starts to fail them. It is a hard fall when you have based your life counting on your physical body. Often seniors respond, when asked, "How are you feeling?" "Oh, everything hurts, and what doesn't hurt, doesn't work."

Some say that this deterioration of our physical bodies is a universal law of returning to source. We have expanded and now we are contracting. This is the birth/death process that is in all living things. In fact, 300 million cells in our bodies are being replaced every minute.

The physical is always changing, decomposing. It makes one wonder if the physical is dependable at all. Physical things are not permanent, and we need something permanent on which to base our lives. Gary Renard in his two books, *Disappearance of the Universe*, and *Your Immortality; and Breaking the Cycle of Birth and Death*, calls the physical an illusion and not a reality. An illusion ultimately can't be trusted; it will change. A reality will be true and forever. Our weather looks like a reality in the moment, but can we count on it to be stable? Can we count on our cars to be maintenance-free? Can we count on people not to get sick? Can we count on our water heater to last much longer than its warranty? Everything physical changes.

Hanya Shingyo, the Buddhist Wisdom and Heart Sutra states, "That which can be seen has no form. That which cannot be seen has form." This quote is similar to Zen Buddhist koans, which are teaching tools used to break down one's resistance to enlightenment. An explanation could be: we can see it so it has no absolute form, because it is physical and always changing. That which we cannot see (Principles and Truths) have form because they do not change. They are reliable.

The documentary film, What the BLEEP Do We Know!?, explains scientifically what appears stable physically to us is always moving and changing. The film was first released in 2004 in Yelm, Washington, and was distributed by its producers. In 2004-05, it won awards in all the five film festivals that it was able to enter. It shows that there is a "market for spiritually oriented films that caters to audiences' intelligence, not their lowest common denominator."[1]

In the film, renowned quantum physicists illustrated how a "solid" (like a table) is actually constantly moving and alive with energy. Everything is energy and alive. I had to chuckle when I got a call from my daughter who wanted to know what I had told my 10 year old grandson about rocks "moving." They had not seen The BLEEP... about the energy and aliveness in all things.

The BLEEP... informs us that the energy of the table is the same energy as in our own molecular structure. Not only are we the same as other living things (plants and animals) in this regard but also with "non-living" physical things. An "out of the box" example of this reality is seen in the practices of Dr. Ihaleakala Hew Len of Hawaii, who has successfully used the Hawaiian healing system called Ho'oponopono. In *zero limits*, Dr. Len tells of his (shamanistic) practices used in conjunction with his workshops. He talks to the room and the chairs beforehand to ascertain their state of being and to gain their permission to hold the workshop. He gives a specific example.[2]

> I was in an auditorium once getting ready to do a lecture, and I was talking to the chairs. I asked, 'Is there anybody I've missed? Does anyone have a problem that I need to take care of?' One of the chairs said, 'You know, there was a guy sitting on me today during a previous seminar who had financial problems, and now I just feel dead!' So I cleaned (using the Ho'oponopono healing method) with that problem, and I could just see the chair straightening up. Then I heard, 'Okay! I'm ready to handle the next guy!'

Could it be that even physical objects respond to appreciation as people do? Dr. Len's respect for physical objects has made me more aware and more appreciative of the physical "beings" around me.

Quantum physicists tell us that all physical is composed of more space than solid, and that the spaces are more important because that is where the energy is. Profoundly, Eckhart Tolle in his book, *The New Earth,* points out that the essence of our "Being" is found in spaces between our thoughts. He urges us to quiet our thoughts and listen to our higher self, which has its home in the spaces. He encourages us to be aware of our breath and experience a state of just "Being." Our deepest self has nothing to do with outer physical identifications -- with roles and titles -- but with our consciousness, our awareness. Here again, the profound is found in the spaces within all, not in the solid of the physical.

No wonder the wolf blew down the house of the pig that valued the physical. The physical is not the foundation on which to build your life. The physical cannot stand the test of timelessness; it changes and is unstable.

Money

In the house of the second pig, the picture on the wall showed a pig surrounded by big gunnysacks with $$ signs on them. The second pig valued money.

Can we base our lives on money, and what that will bring? If so, all people who are "rich" would be exceedingly stable and happy. How flawed is that? Many who won the lottery did not live happily ever after. Money issues are a main cause of failing marriages, and it doesn't matter how much money the couple has. Money allows us to have more choices, but it can't serve as the basis for a happy and meaningful life.

The illusion that money and more money will bring security and increase our happiness is an illusion that is held by most Americans. It's an example of basing one's life on a belief that is not true. People try to gain what they really need by expensive substitutes. There are no absolutes; a given object may seem like a fulfillment to one, but not another. People are really looking for a true, deep sense of fulfillment, a feeling. That cannot be gained by physical, outer things.

This does not mean that people who are wealthy cannot be happy and fulfilled, but it is not because they have money. Money can be a deterrent to happiness, because it may keep a person focusing outward instead of inward, where the true treasures are. As you will see in later chapters, those attributes such as inner peace, fulfillment, meaning, and happiness are gained in entirely different ways than having money.

People want expansion in their lives, but they look for it in an outer way versus an inner way. They really want depth. Dr. Viktor Frankl, World War II concentration camp survivor said, "If you don't go within, you are simply without." I see this as saying, if you don't go with the inner, you are simply without.

Bhagavan Sri Sathya Sai Baba reminds us:[3]

> Man feels that riches are paramount, but what he fancies as wealth are but material, momentary, trivial things. Character, virtue, brotherhood, charity -- these are the real riches. The company of the good and godly is the wealth that that is most worthy. Wisdom is the most precious wealth. The educated person must live with this conviction. Search for mere riches can never confer contentment and peace of mind. Each one yearns for lasting joy but does not stop to discover from where it can be got. It is not available anywhere outside him.

Neale Donald Walsch, in *Communion with God*, tells of the 10 Illusions of Humans. The first is the Illusion of Need; the nine that follow are based on it. All the problems in the world might be boiled down to that first illusion. People think they need "things" to make them happy -- the car, the boat, the house, the job, the trip, the "soul mate." If one believes in the illusion of Need, these follow: Failure, Disunity, Insufficiency, Requirement, Judgment, Condemnation, Conditionality, Superiority, and Ignorance. Look at them in reverse to see the ramifications of ignorance.

Neale Donald Walsch states in his trilogy, *Conversations with God*, that the correct flow is "Be Do Have" not "Have Do Be." People mistakenly think they must Have something, to be able to Do something, in order to Be (happy). But it is the reverse. When one comes from a place of Being (thankfulness, happiness), one is able to Do things in the right way, then Have things that are fulfilling. It is flowing with the Universe, with the Universal Principles and Truths.

Beings. Human Beings. Are we acting more like humans than beings? Perhaps. "Human" certainly has a bad connotation to it. When someone does something wrong, it is said, "it's just 'human nature'." Perhaps we need to focus on our positive "being" nature.

Neale Donald Walsch's question to all of us in *The New Revelations*:

> (We) must collectively ask:
>
> Is this who we are? Is this who we choose to be? Is this the only way we can live? Is this the only way we know how to behave? Is it possible there might be another way?
>
> Might this other way bring us closer to what we say, as a species, that we really want? Are we missing something here? Do we have the courage to seriously look at what that might be? Do we have the courage to accept the answer that our searching uncovers?

Our nation and people are in such illusion about what brings happiness in life that we live with "phantom wealth." Many households do not really own what possessions they have, but have charged them and are in credit card debt. According to the U.S. National Debt Clock, the United States National Debt is $10,633 trillion as of January 31, 2009, and with the population being 305,563,681, each citizen's share of this debt is $34,798. Since September 28, 2007, the debt has continued to increase an average of $3.31 billion per day! More than a trillion dollars will be added to it with loans to banks and car manufacturers that have failed, and with the government stimulus packages hoping to put people back to work. Personally and collectively we are living in illusion when we are in debt and don't own what we have "free and clear."

Money can be an addiction; there never seems to be enough. It can lead a person, a business, a nation and a world into chaos. Addiction is the cause of the financial chaos that broke out September/October 2008, when the results of years of greed and corruption became evident. Big business was already addicted to money; salaries, bonuses and golden parachutes were measured not in terms of thousands, but in millions. We have seen that lenders sold risky housing loans. Mesmerized banks bought them. Unaffordable loans defaulted and foreclosures ensued. Banks defaulted, causing other businesses to default, leading to unemployment. Cities lost income, became insolvent, and some went bankrupt.

All areas of the economy are affected. My husband's and my retirement pensions from The University of California, one of the biggest and most reliable educational institutions, feels the pressure on their pension and retiree health programs, and warns that changes will be coming.[4]

I did not expect or desire to have an even more personal and glaring example of the effects of corruption and greed to detail in this book. I have been handling our personal investments more than 25 years and have taken many subscriptions and programs for advice, but none like the group of advisors I encountered from February 2009 to October 2009. They promised me a personalized service, and it was, at first. Then, after getting me into one of their most expensive services, which they touted as the most personalized, they stopped calling me with advisories.

When I called them, they were always "out to lunch," or "busy on another call." The receptionist advised me to send them an email, which I did. It did not elicit any response, except from the receptionist when I called in again, saying that I was "complaining." After sending in a more detailed email, the receptionist told me I no longer had a personal representative. They stopped my service, which was supposed to continue for seven more months.

I reported them to the Attorney General's Office in New York City, the Securities and Exchange Commission, and various on-line complaint boards because of their misleading advertising and not delivering as promised. That being done, I shifted my negative attitude to one of forgiveness toward them and for myself for this hard learned lesson. On April 20, 2010, the owner and president of the firm and four other employees were arrested for securities and wire fraud. If convicted, the five suspects face up to 20 years in prison.[5] Poor customer service was the least of their transgressions. The charges included setting up deceptively false addresses and telephone numbers for the firm and fictitious trading experts. There was nothing credible about this firm.

"Stefan Theil (in an article in the Foreign Policy magazine) concluded that Europe, particularly France and Germany, are teaching their children...that capitalism is immoral, savage and unhealthy."[6] We might have questioned that before October 2008, but as examples of greed and corruption were exposed almost daily, it caused one to wonder.

World economies were affected because of trade and currency balances. Europe had a right to be concerned. The British Broadcasting Company's business editor Robert Preston stated:[7]

> ...that we are seeing a massive flight of capital out of economies perceived to have been living beyond their means - either because they have a substantial reliance on foreign borrowings or because they are net importers of good and services, or both.

The IMF (International Monetary Fund) reported,[8]

> ...financial markets remain under stress and the global economy has taken a 'sharp turn for the worse.' 'We now expect the global economy to come to a virtual halt,' said IMF chief economist Olivier Blanchard.... ...the International Labour Organization said that as many as 51 million jobs worldwide could be lost this year because of the global economic crisis. ...Countries such as China are now struggling with a collapse in demand from their primary export markets. Meanwhile, developed economies such as Japan, Spain, the US and UK are in recession, with new job losses being announced on a daily basis.

Alan Greenspan, Chairman of the Federal Reserve from 1987-2006 admitted that he had put too much faith in the self-correcting power of free markets.[9] In other words, he expected people to self-regulate and not be so greedy and corrupt.

The pig's house built on money didn't survive either. We really desire depth, true security, and true wealth, not just money. "True wealth is the awareness of Spirit." (Jim Rosemergy). "Wealth isn't how much money you have, it's what you're left with if you lose all your money." (Roger Hamilton)

Security does not come from having money. It comes from the inner, an attitude, Being, which is based on understanding and living in harmony with Universal Principles and Spiritual Truths.

People

Inside the third house is a picture on the wall of a pig surrounded by other little pigs. This house is the key to the illusion of many well-intentioned people. Albeit positive relationships with others are important, but is it a strong enough foundation to base one's life on?

What happens when your loved one goes away to college, or your spouse divorces you or dies? Will people always be there for you, to protect you, guide you, love you, understand and listen to you? There are many negatives that can be generated when you have a dependency on people, especially when they don't live up to your expectations – you feel hurt, blame, anger, fear, regret, resentment or disappointment. The difference between being alone and being lonely is linked to this issue of dependency on people. People are to be given to, not to be expected from.

Neale Donald Walsch gives us some thoughts about one's right relationship to people.[10]

> Spend the rest of your life giving people back to themselves, that they might love themselves. And show them by how you are with them that you know there is nothing they are lacking, nothing they are missing, nothing they need, nothing they are not.

Might this answer our question, is it about playing the game of life in competition with others, or only in comparison with ourselves?

This excerpt from The Peace Prayer of St. Francis is also clarifying.[11]

> Lord, make me an instrument of your peace.
> Where there is hatred, let me sow love.
> Where there is injury, pardon.
> Where there is doubt, faith.
> Where there is despair, hope.
> Where there is darkness, light.
> And where there is sadness, joy.
>
> O Divine Master, grant that
> I may not so much seek
> to be consoled as to console;
> to be understood as to understand;
> to be loved as to love...

We feel separate from other people. Indeed, most experience this when we are not understood, when we don't feel loved by others. We do have an interrelationship with others, but physically, we are separate. It has been said that we are born alone and we die alone.

To realize that we are really alone, that we are free from being dependent on other people, can bring great strength of character. Through this solitude, one can accept and glean from one's own experiences. You have to trust in yourself. You have to have that kind of being to investigate the deeper parts of life and yourself, to be open to your own ideas, your own insights, as well as those of others. People who only accept the outer, physical world (what they can see, touch, hear, feel and smell) may think you are a little strange if your interest is in more than the physical. Even in the early stages of many inventors' lives, they were thought to be somewhat crazy.

I remember the day very well when, in my 30s, I realized that I was alone, even though my mom and dad were still alive, and I had a loving husband and two children. I think the realization was shocking and powerful because it came on quickly, and I had no idea what caused it. I had been over protected as a child, and I considered myself to be more dependant than most.

That one particular morning, I woke up and was immediately depressed with the realization that I was alone. I didn't want to get out of bed. I felt immobilized. I was in shock. Luckily it was on a weekend, and my husband was home to help with our two pre-school children. I remember him semi-dragging me out of bed, saying we were going to the park. I went because I was afraid to be alone if I didn't go with them. I was like a zombie and felt like I was on a different planet. I was experiencing that I was alone, and no one really cared about me. My family did, but not really. It was deeper than that. I realized I was totally responsible, in control of my life and could not depend on anyone. It took a couple of days, but I began to accept the reality of aloneness. It was a maturing realization and acceptance, because it made me less dependent on what others thought or said, and strong enough to think for myself. It started me on a path of accepting myself.

In The Mystery Plays by Roberto Aguirre-Sacasa, Mister Mystery states "We are all of us alone. Our lives, our paths, we walk alone even when surrounded by our families and our friends. We are alone." Sylvia Browne, spiritual teacher and psychic, states in many of her books that we each plan our own Life Path, the learning experiences we want to experience to further perfect our soul. We plan these on the Other Side before coming into this lifetime. No one person's path is like another. We are indeed alone, different and separate from others, on our own path.

This concept is reiterated in the philosophy of Numerology, an ancient science developed by Pythagoras, which states again that we plan our distinctive Life Path, which is derived from our date of birth. Our birth date is not a coincidence, but carefully planned by us before we were born because we wanted to walk a certain path while on Earth.

Spiritualists say we have interdimensional beings with us all the time. What we call "our guides" may not be something separate from us at all however, but a part of our own being that was split off when we were born into a human form. No wonder they are so supportive and loving.

How do we get to the position of expecting less from people? As we begin to open up to the magnificence and love from our higher selves/the All/God, we look less to people for love. A higher dimension is the true source that enables us to give to people rather than asking or expecting something from them. The equation will begin to reverse itself when one feels the higher love. This is the secret exposed by the third house of the little pigs, how to be in a right relationship with people.

The third house reveals that a stable, solid and secure life is not to be based on a dependency on people, because even though this house withstood the huff and puff of the wolf, we shall soon see that this house was still vulnerable.

The three little pigs challenge us to think about what we are basing our lives on currently. The pictures on the walls were the keys to the pigs' values. Even today, I look at pictures on the walls of homes to get to know the people. What do the pictures in your home reveal about you? What do you value? Something stable? Something timeless? What are we attached to -- the Physical, Money, Our Family, Friends? Are we really secure?

Consider the Universal Principles and Spiritual Truths; they always were, always are, and always will be. They are the stable foundation, worthy to build your life on.

PRINCIPLE #2:
WHAT DO YOU DO WHEN EVIL GETS IN YOUR HOUSE?

The second major principle in *The Three Little Pigs* has to do with the subject of evil and how to handle it. The wolf in this story is a symbol for evil. In the original story, the wolf blows down two of the three houses, but he wasn't able to blow down the third. However, the last house was still vulnerable because people can't bring stability to your life. This wolf was crafty; he decided to get in by coming down the chimney.

Even if you have a strong house and a strong foundation, evil can happen to you. The third pig was not frozen by fear; he was resourceful and thought ahead. He put on a pot of water to boil in the fireplace. When the wolf came down the chimney, he landed in the pot. Then the three pigs ate the wolf for dinner.

What happened to the wolf is one of the most misunderstood, yet profound parts of *The Three Little Pigs* story. In most of the later versions, the wolf is shown running away. What most don't realize is that this story is symbolic. The story attempts to transmit a Universal Principle and Spiritual

Truth. The story is not showing violence to animals; this is too literal an interpretation of a symbolic story.

This story shows that even the strong brick house had flaws. The outer flaw was the chimney that the wolf could enter. The inner flaw was the dependency on people. The issue here is, however, no matter how strong a house one has, no matter how righteous or spiritual one's being and actions are, the wolf will get in. One will experience "evil" some time in one's life. There are books written about why "bad" things happen to "good" people, and superstitions about "bad" things happening because one is a "bad" person.

When our son was four years old, he was hit and run over by a car. He was in a critical condition for two weeks. During that time, we got an anonymous letter in the mail, poorly handwritten in poor English, telling us that what had happened to our son was because we were evil people, and we had caused the accident. I threw the letter away without fully reading it, knowing it was not true in any way.

Eating the wolf symbolically means internalizing evil, accepting evil. This may sound a bit jarring, but many psychologists and spiritualists have written that acceptance is needed to heal anything -- acceptance that it happened, that it was.

Take a look at the negative emotion of anger. It results from not being able to accept that something happened. Is that crazy? Accept that it happened. This does not mean that you have to like it.

Keys to resolving anger with another person are accepting that it did happen, then forgiveness and compassion. The truth is that you are always in charge and you can change your attitude, so the issue is with yourself, not the other person. If you understand that, you will be able to turn anger into forgiveness and compassion.

"TUT...A Note from the Universe" states: [1]

> Young souls get angry at others.
> Old souls get angry at themselves.
> But really wise souls have already turned the page.
> Got forever and ever?

There is an acceptance, devoid of fear, anger and other negative emotions, that is needed before one can see clearly. The third pig accepted the predicament, moved beyond any fear that would cause immobilization, and was therefore able to take creative action.

Elizabeth Kubler-Ross' book *On Death and Dying* tells us that acceptance is the last and final step in healing. This is an important process, because accepting death is the same issue as accepting anything one would consider evil or bad.

Oprah Winfrey's TV show aired a story about a woman who, just after her second child's birth, and while still in the hospital, was infected with flesh-eating bacteria. Because of this, she lost several internal organs and both of her arms and legs. In spite of all this, she had an amazing attitude. She had focused on getting home to her children. She did have moments of sadness when she realized she would not be able to hold her newborn daughter, but she did not dwell on regret, anger, blame, or other negatives about her condition.

She did not resist the evil; she accepted it. What happened to her just was. In spite of her physical disabilities, she was able to have a positive attitude that was a blessing for all. Abraham-Hicks (Abraham, channeled by Esther Hicks) calls this "The Law of Allowing" and "The Law of Detachment."

Jesus of Nazareth according to the Bible, Matthew 5:39, said, "Resist not evil." He was warning about fighting evil. Acknowledge that it was and accept it. This will release you to respond in a creative way.

In *zero limits*, Dr. Hew Len, master of the Ho'oponopono healing process, said:[2]

> What we humans are unaware of in our moment-to-moment existence is a constant, incessant resistance to life. This resistance keeps us in a constant, incessant state of displacement from our Self-I-Dentity and from Freedom, Inspiration, and above all else the Divine Creator itself. Simply put, we are displaced people wandering aimlessly in the desert of our minds. ... Resistance keeps us in a constant state of anxiety and spiritual, mental, physical, financial, and material impoverishment.

Outcomes are different when they come from acceptance rather than resistance. When someone gives you advice about something, you can tell if the advice comes from a state of resistance or acceptance. If the advice comes from a resistant state, there may be an undertone of a condescending nature. With an attitude of acceptance, the person's tone has understanding and compassion.

In Buddhism, The Four Noble Truths say that all Life is Suffering. That Suffering is caused by Attachment. Our call is to end the Suffering. The key is to give up the Attachment or the Desire -- an emotion and feeling, which is emotionally charged and clouds our vision and actions.

Neale Donald Walsch says to "stop the stopping." It follows that any protest that is anti-anything is giving power to the negative and becomes counter productive. Therefore, join a march for peace rather than an anti-war march.

I use the "resist not" principle to stop my headaches. When I start to get one, I sit down right away and describe it to myself. What color is it? How hard or soft? With this acceptance, I am able to stop the headache in a short time.

Do you think you are tired more than you should be? If so, look into your levels of resistance. This does not have to be in the obvious levels of hate, anger, and hurt. Look into the more subtle, everyday happenings in the range of disappointments, feeling overwhelmed, concerns, unfulfilled wishes, anything that keeps you from being grateful and thankful in the moment. "Rest seems like a nice contrast to overwhelment (sic), but enthusiasm is always chosen over rest. The only thing that ever makes you tired or bogs you down is resistance."[3]

It is a natural tendency to fight against something we don't want, but fighting only makes things worse and gives it power. Carl Jung reminds us: "What you resist, persists. What you fight you get more of."

Fighting instead of accepting causes resistance, which causes stress. When you are stressed, your immune system is suppressed. If you are stressed for a substantial length of time, your body can become diseased (dis-eased).

I had breast cancer, and I know I caused it. In my mid-50s, I was so stressed and in psychological pain that I became suicidal. Cancer cells are with us all the time. They are cells that do not function, yet they circulate in our body waiting for a chance to take over and multiply. Our immune system usually takes care of them, but when stress suppresses our immune system, the cancer cells have a chance to take a foothold. I counsel women with breast cancer. I ask them, what happened to you six months ago? Invariably, they were experiencing a high degree of stress. Dr. Wayne Dyer reminds us, "Row, row, row your boat, gently, down the stream." The emphasis is on gently and down, not vigorously and up. Go with the flow.

We stayed at a golf resort in Arizona in 2007, and on one of the walls was a picture, which immediately amazed me with its symbology.

I saw a story of choosing either a path of accepting reality and being in the flow of life, or resisting it. Starting from right to left: we are before the physical, deciding and reaching to come into the physical. The circled dot, the circumpunct, has various meanings and among them is the "eye of God."

When we become physical, we have two roads we can follow. The higher road reaches out to us and welcomes us to travel there in the divine flow (acceptance, non-resistance of evil), the opposite of resisting. This higher ground leads one to the possibility for respect of all living things, seeing that God is in all things. The result is enlightenment. Then one is liberated from a physical preoccupation and negativity. One becomes free and an open channel, focused upward to receive divine inspiration.

If one rejects the upper path, on the lower, one is jerked around, up and down, by one's resistance and negativity to all that happens. This is a dead end where one becomes caught in the physical, a prisoner of one's own mind, with thoughts based in non-truths and ego, trapped. In *The New Earth*, Eckhart Tolle also talks about constrictions of the mind and the ego versus becoming acquainted with our true being and essence.

In writing this book, I discovered several books about writing, which I normally would not have read. In *Finding Water,* Julia Cameron talks about the issue of creativity, a must for writers. She said, "Creativity flourishes in an atmosphere of acceptance." Indeed, everything flourishes in acceptance, and that is why negative emotions limit us so. The forms of resistance block us from our true potential.

If you think resistance is a pattern you want to understand and eliminate in yourself, how do you go about it? The first step in anything is to become aware. Resistance shows up as anger, hurt, worry, regret, fear, guilt and a variety of similar negative emotions. It is also a component of depression and wanting to sleep more than is needed. Remember that most of our actions are habits that we have developed, and if we created them, we can release them. Often the resistance appears because we are holding a belief that is not true. Maybe we are basing our lives on something that is not reliable, like the false values that handicapped the pigs.

When one of these negatives appear, ask yourself, what am I resisting? What is the basis of my thought? Even though I might not like what happened, did it happen? Yes, it did; and my feelings will not erase it. So, free yourself by accepting it, and move on to respond.

The little pigs have given us a valuable clue to winning the game of life. Eat the wolf. Accept. Detach. Resist not. This profound principle will challenge you as much as, if not more than, any outer accomplishment in your life.

As the three little pigs have shown us, if we can't find stability and base our lives on the physical, money, status, our job and title, other people and a myriad of other "seen" things, what can we base our lives on? What is reliable and will not change? What can we trust? What will bring true security? What is true? On what can we base our decisions and actions?

You will see; there is an answer.

HOW DO WE KNOW WHAT IS TRUE?

The Three Little Pigs unlocked the door, opened it, and found the lost principles -- building our lives on something everlasting, and how to handle evil. This leads us to search for more Universal Principles and Spiritual Truths (the rules of the game of life). But before we do that, we need to discover our own perceptions about truth. What do we already think is true? How do how we evaluate whether something is true when we find it?

Most of the time we base our lives on concepts and ideas that we are not conscious of, and perhaps not true. Psychologists say that only one-sixth of our psyche is conscious. We most often base our beliefs and actions on the values and beliefs of our parents or primary caretakers, what they have told us about ourselves, others, and the world. If we do not examine them, we are not the masters of our own lives.

We are challenged to examine our beliefs so as to live our lives based on truth.[1]

> The time has come for you to have more courage than any war has ever called upon you for, than

any hardship has ever demanded, than even
suffering has ever required. The time has come
for you to confront yourself at the level of belief.
The reason this will require so much courage is
that your beliefs form the basis of who you think
you are.

You must challenge yourself.
You must challenge your society.
You must challenge your world.

Harry Rathbun, one of the originators of The Creative Initiative Foundation, said not to sit on a chair that is not there. The chair needs to be a reality. There are instances where, at first, we may not be sure how a principle will work in a particular situation, but we still can have faith that the principle is true. That is sitting on a chair that is there.

According to the Bible, Jesus of Nazareth says how important it is to base your life on truth, the foundation of your house.[2]

> He is like a man which (sic) built a house, and
> digged (sic) deep, and laid the foundation on a
> rock: and when the flood arose, the stream beat
> vehemently upon that house, and could not shake
> it: for it was founded upon a rock. But the one who
> has heard and has not acted accordingly, is like a
> man who built a house on the ground without any
> foundation; and the torrent burst against it and
> immediately it collapsed, and the ruin of that
> house was great.

Byron Katie's questions in her book, *Loving What Is: Four Questions That Can Change Your Life,* lead us to examine beliefs that we think are true and see if they really are. She asks, "Would you rather be right or free?"[3] I remember my parents indirectly saying and acting as if I was not able to handle most situations by myself. I should be cautious and careful, and never broach the subjects of politics and religion. As I matured, I painstakingly climbed out of that dependency prison.

After recently reading Katie's book and applying her questions to these particular beliefs, I found remnants of the old beliefs persisted. And, I was continually working against them. The belief they implied (and that I unconsciously accepted) that I was not able, was entirely false. I am able. I felt a new sense of freedom after realizing that limitation, and claiming what was really true.

More and more scientists are starting to investigate the power of our minds. Dan Brown in his 2009 book, *The Lost Symbol*, mentions Noetic Science. In Petaluma, CA, there is The Institute of Noetic Science (IONS), which is a non-profit membership organization that conducts and sponsors leading-edge research into the potentials and powers of consciousness.[4] They are doing groundbreaking work in studying how ideas can be transmitted to bring about reality.

Dr. William A. Tiller, Fellow to the American Academy for the Advancement of Science, and Professor Emeritus of Stanford University's Department of Materials Science states:[5]

> For the last four hundred years, an unstated assumption of science is that human intention cannot affect what we call "physical reality." Our experimental research of the past decade shows that, for today's world and under the right conditions, this assumption is no longer correct. We humans are much more than we think we are and Psychoenergetic Science continues to expand the proof of it.

Dr. Tiller spent 34 years in academia after nine years as an advisory physicist with the Westinghouse Research Laboratories. He has published more than 250 conventional scientific papers, 3 books and several patents. In parallel, for over 30 years, he has been avocationally pursuing serious experimental and theoretical study in the field of psychoenergetics, which will likely become an integral part of "tomorrow's" physics. In this new area, he has published an additional 100 scientific papers and four seminal books.

True maturity has nothing to do with age, but an attitude about truth. The truly mature person is able to listen to all ideas, not being attached to his or her own. It is a state of detachment to be able to admit that one may not know the whole truth and be open to other possibilities. Yet, psychologists tell us that one of the most difficult things to do is to change one's thoughts about something. An enlightened approach, when one comes across a different point of view, might be to think how it could be true vs. thinking how it is false.

One definition of what it means to be mature is the ability to entertain one's self, entertain another person, and entertain an idea. To entertain rather than resist another's idea makes conversations with others much more enjoyable and welcoming.

Admitting that you are wrong about something may be more threatening than changing a habit or practice. It is easy to become attached to one's beliefs without even knowing it. What happens with your feelings when someone expresses a belief different than yours, or challenges yours in some way. It's a key to how attached you are to your belief. Are you quick to defend? Are you interested in their different point of view? Do you find that you are so quick to challenge, that sometimes you interrupt them before they finish their thought?

The views of others may add valuable information, opening up our blind areas. Often it is what we don't know that controls us, not what we know. As a diagram, what is known by another may help uncover what is unknown by me.

	KNOWN BY ME	*UNKNOWN BY ME*
KNOWN BY ANOTHER	OPEN	*BLIND*
UNKNOWN BY ANOTHER	HIDDEN	UNKNOWN

We bring others into our lives through synchronicity. There is a reason they are there. They are our teachers.

"Lay of the Higher Law," an excerpt from the Sufi Kasidah of Haji Abdu El-Yezdi, states:[6]

> Truth is the shattered mirror
> Strewn in myriad bits.
> Each believes that his little bit
> Is the whole truth.

In the *Tales of the Dervishes, Teaching Stories of the Sufi Masters over the Past Thousand Years* by Idries Shah, there is the story "The Blind Ones and the Matter of the Elephant." There was a community of blind men who were explaining what an elephant looked like to the rest of the blind population. When they were asked about form, the one that felt an ear likened the animal to a rug. The one who felt the trunk said he had the real facts; the animal was like a pipe. Another said the elephant was like pillars, after feeling only the legs. They all thought they knew the truth about the elephant, although each of them had only felt one part of it.

Often, we are likened to the blind ones when it comes to the total truth about something. We all have our own "frame of reference," our own bias, our own "vested interest" and our own "rose colored glasses." The Talmud states: "We do not see things as they are. We see them as we are."
Everyone thinks they see the truth but our eyes can deceive us. Criminologists tell us that eyewitnesses are among the least reliable for crime scene facts. We can be well intentioned, but many times what we see or hear is not the whole truth.

What do you see in the following picture?

Camel Caravan, Wadi Mitan   ©George Steinmetz

Camels in the desert? Yes and No. Most apparent are the dark shapes. However, the dark shapes are really the shadows of the camels. One has to look closely to see that the real camels are the little white objects at the feet of the shadows. This example is to remind us not to be too quick to evaluate and judge. What one sees at first in a situation or thought, may not be the true or complete reality.

Neale Donald Walsch wrote of the biggest fallacies about God and Life.[7]

> Humanity's major fallacies about God and about Life make for a deadly litany of error that has created, and continues to create to this very moment, a world of deep anger, brutal violence, terrible loss, unrelenting sorrow, and unremitting terror.... You think other people are terrorizing you, but in truth you are being terrorized by your (own) beliefs.

It is important that our beliefs are based in truth because who we are and our actions spring from our beliefs. Buddha, Hindu Prince Gautama Siddharta, the founder of Buddhism, 563-483 B.C., said, "All that we are is the result of what we have thought. The mind is everything. What we think we become." And Marcus Aurelius, AD 121-180, Roman Emperor, who was often referred to as "the wise," said, "A man's life is what his thoughts make of it."

Truth is not normal in many everyday dealings. Take politics, for instance. As with political elections of the past, in the Fall of 2008, it was difficult to determine "the truth, the whole truth, and nothing but the truth." Perhaps those who wrote the television advertisements thought it was OK to bend the truth or err by omission, because they were not on the stand testifying. It would be cumbersome, but it would be interesting if all ads would have to stand the scrutiny of the courts before being broadcast. (At least pharmaceutical ads give the downside to the drug, even if while listening it seems that the downside might be more of a problem that the original condition.)

There were many half-truths in the election information. But what is a half-truth anyway? It doesn't deserve to have the word "truth" associated with it. It's not true in any way if it is just "half."

Especially with the TV ads for the Propositions, much was taken out of context and exaggerated. If one was concerned about accuracy, one could look at who sponsored the ad, if you could figure out who belonged to that group that you had never heard of before. And, you can't always trust what you get on the Internet. I felt really embarrassed when I found out that one political "fact" that I had sent to several of my friends was completely fraudulent. Also, one can never be sure who the author of the Internet information really is.

A strong test of truth is: does it ring true with your experience? Those who have lived longer may have an advantage, having more time to test the validity of something. This is not always the case however. You have a chance to test the validity of what you read here to see if it is compatible with your life experience.

You may be given a clue that something is very true when it gives you chills. This is communication from the deepest and highest parts of your self. It is a real aid in discovering or confirming important truths. I urge you to pay attention and revisit those concepts if this has happened to you while reading.

What Is True About The Game Of Life?

In this book, we are looking specifically for the truths about life, the rules of the game. We can discover these with study, reading books or listening to talks by spiritual and metaphysical teachers. You can examine your own experiences and try to learn from them. Some receive information through intuition, meditation and psychic powers. No one method is better than another; it has to do with personal preference and abilities. Most use more than one method.

After I started my search for Universal Principles, I began to discover that these did seem to be the rules of the game of life. They included information about who we are as human beings, the nature of our world, and the energies within and around us. They incorporated physical, mental, emotional and spiritual aspects. I refer to these rules as Universal Principles and Spiritual Truths.

Moses had the right idea about there being rules, but rules in the negative only bring about negative (thou shalt not...). We need guidelines on what we shalt. The Principles and Truths are objective, neither negative nor positive. The "shalt" is to live in harmony with them.

By the end of the 1980s, my search for these truths led me to discover only two Universal Principles. By 2008, my list had grown to over 30. I refined and consolidated them to nine. I include many references from people of different ethnicities and disciplines who give their own unique viewpoints.

In Part I, we looked at two Universal Principles in the little pigs' story -- what to build your life on and how to handle evil. In the following chapters, I will expand on those truths, and list and combine additional Principles and Truths from my original 30. This book does not claim to present original concepts, or to be the final word on this subject.

Neale Donald Walsch challenges us:[8]

> Never stop doubting, never stop questioning, never. Never assume you have all the answers. Having all the answers kills the question itself; renders it lifeless—and you too. Keep looking, keep seeking. Never, ever find it all. Because when you find it all, you deny that there is more. And there is never not more.

Universal Principles and Spiritual Truths have helped me immensely in my life. The principles and truths are so practical. It enables one to see the essence, the core of a situation, and how to resolve anything one might consider a problem. On the humorous side, when an issue comes up, I often say to myself, "Oh, that's principle number eight." Sometimes I also say "That's the third house of the little pigs."

When one understands the Principles and Truths, things in life become much clearer. There are certain words that will be eliminated from your vocabulary: happenstance, accident, magic, luck, and coincidence. There is a cause-and-effect predictability and order in the Universe. In *Conversations with God*:[9]

> I tell you this: There is no coincidence, and nothing happens "by accident." Each event and adventure is called to your Self by your Self in order that you might create and experience Who You Really Are. All true Masters know this. That is why mystic Masters remain unperturbed in the face of the worst experiences of life (as you would define them).

Eckhart Tolle reminds us in his book, *The New Earth*, that even the word cosmos means order. Most often we just see the effects and are ignorant of the cause. The key to the cause lies in the Principles and Truths.

I remembered the story of *The Three Little Pigs* when I heard an interesting perspective on levels of consciousness in people. On the first level, people concern themselves with other people -- who they are, what they are doing and what they have. On the second level, current and past events hold most interest. On the highest level, people concern themselves with principles.

The three little pigs were trying to build their houses (their lives) on something that is true, forever and sturdy. They needed to know about Universal Principles and Spiritual Truths.

The pigs would have eliminated a lot of effort and stress if they valued and knew to establish their houses on the guidelines of principles and truths. The deepest understanding is never the outer, what they built their houses with. It is the inner, what was in their houses. Perhaps the pigs would have been more secure if the pictures inside their houses would have been sayings of Principles and Truths vs. pictures of muscular pigs, moneyed pigs, and other pigs.

Knowing and practicing these principles can enable you, as well as the pigs, to live in reality and stability. They are the rules of life, the key to claiming your birthright -- to eliminate negativity and to live with love, inner peace, understanding, gratitude and thankfulness, no matter what happens to you or others.

Life is an amazing journey. Life does make sense.

ALL EXISTS IN DUALITY

Duality was one of the first Universal Principles I discovered, and this concept made a profound impact on my life. Many more opposites will be introduced in the principles that follow because duality is woven into the matrix of life. It is a truth you can count on.

The Yin Yang is an ancient Taoist symbol of the interplay and inseparable interrelationship of light and dark forces in the universe. The Yin (dark) is the passive, negative, receptive, a female source. The Yang (light) is the active, positive, movement, a male source. The S-like curve symbolizes the dance of the energies; that nothing is absolute in itself, but changing, fluid and active. Even in the dark side there is a hint of the white, and the white has a hint of the dark, showing the complexity and interrelationship between the two.

What side of the Yin Yang are you on most of the time? The idea is not to be a Pollyanna (all positive) or Draconian (all negative). There is always a balance, but we may not be aware how much we live on the negative side. What if part of the reason we came to Earth was to learn how to resolve negativity? Thinking negatively affects our beliefs, actions health, and that of others.

Other than the most obvious negative states (hate, regret, blame, guilt), there are two that are common and deserve some time here because they are so debilitating and habitual. Worry and fear. They are closely interrelated. If you fear something, you are likely to worry about it, and visa versa. What are worry and fear, really? Negative thinking about something that hasn't happened yet. The future is still neutral. Why think negatively; why not be positive?

The Internet message "I Believe God Wants You to Know" states:[1]

> ...that fear is one of the main sources of cruelty. To conquer fear is the beginning of wisdom.
> Bertrand Russell said that, and he was right.
>
> Elisabeth Kubler-Ross said, "Fear and guilt are the only enemies of man." She was right, too.
>
> And Franklin Roosevelt famously said, "We have nothing to fear but fear itself."

Worry and fear are both states of resistance. They keep a person from being able to think or see clearly. *They are not an indication that you care about someone.* In fact, they may actually be causing a negative to happen because of the Law Attraction, a concept that states, what you think about may cause it to happen. You are a magnet and attract what you think about.

Overcoming fears first involves evaluating if the fear is justifiable or irrational. People can develop irrational fears because of something that happened in their past -- like a fear of balloons, clowns, cotton balls, or bridges. And there are behaviors known as Obsessive/Compulsive Disorders (OCD), when people are compulsive about doing things in a certain order, or cleaning or counting, because if they don't, they fear something bad will happen.

On the other hand, some fears are justifiable. The key is knowledge. For instance, snakes are a justifiable fear; however, some are not deadly. I used to be afraid of all snakes. I think one of the factors was what my mom said to me when something was close by, "If it were a snake, it would have bit you." I am no longer afraid of snakes in general, because I learned about them and found out which ones are really dangerous and which ones aren't.

I was glad I had done my research before that snake bit me. I was in a river, up to my waist in water while fly-fishing. Without looking, I put my hand on a log behind me. A snake bit me, then recoiled back into a hole in the log. Although I was surprised by the bite, I didn't panic, because I saw its head. It was not a rattlesnake, but a harmless garter snake. On the other hand, I have great respect for rattlesnakes.

Often fear and worry are habits, and if you have a fear or tend to worry about something, you may have many fears and many worries. Some years ago, I heard an interesting perspective on the fear of death. The saying was, if you fear death, perhaps you have never really lived.

Is it your desire to see clearly and be responsive in situations versus to be in a frozen and confused state caused by fear and worry? Napoleon Hill advised when you begin to fear, ask yourself "Why am I making this real?"

One way to handle fear and worry is to remind yourself that you are projecting an outcome on something that hasn't happened yet. When I catch myself, I repeatedly tell myself to be present. If the fear or worry is great, the energy that it takes to bring myself back to the present is also great. It may feel like you are fighting a great battle, as great as any physical battle with hand-to-hand combat. This inner battle can leave me exhausted, with an elevated blood pressure, so I am practicing not to let it go to those extremes. Having a symbol is often helpful to remind yourself of a concept. I bought a dramatic ring that I wear to help bring me back "to my senses."

The duality of the Yin Yang shows us that both negative and positive exist. Instead of negativity, such as worry and fear, we can choose to think positively and draw positive to the situation. After all, it hasn't happened yet. It's only in your mind, your belief system. As Buddha reminds us, "All we are is a result of what we have thought."

One of my earliest applications of the Yin Yang duality was that there were masculine and feminine principles in each person. We have an active side and a passive side, a side that talks and a side that listens. In a person, one is usually more predominant than the other. Both are extremely essential.

One of our lessons during our lifetime is to learn to develop the opposite, so as to be functional in both, and whole. Often if you decide to have a significant partner in your life, what you need to be more functional is often found in the other; your challenge is to learn that from him or her. The statements of "he completes me" and "my other half" show a misunderstanding that another person is needed to make you whole. It's one of the dangers illustrated in the third house of the little pigs where there is dependency on other people. We are all whole; the "missing" qualities need to be developed in ourselves. Just this year, a man humorously asked me where my "other half" was. I looked him straight in the eye and said with a smile, "I am whole and he is whole."

In the Gospel of Thomas, 22.b, Jesus affirmed the importance of wholeness.

> …when you make the two into one…and thus make the male and female the same, so that the male isn't male and the female isn't female…, then you will enter the Kingdom.

In my 30s, I had a recurring dream in which I was running around my house, panicked, locking doors and windows just before two "robbers" reached them. Knowing that dreams are our subconscious trying to help us (especially with recurring dreams), I followed the advice of a friend to let the "robbers" in. It took courage to do this, but when I did, I found that these were not robbers but "friends" -- my husband and young son. They said they were there to help me. The masculine principle was my challenge to develop, and they were symbols of the mature masculine and the immature masculine there to help. As soon as I understood this, I never had the dream again.

In linear thinking, everything exists in perceived opposites. (More later about why I qualify that statement.) There are up and down, good and evil, hot and cold, black and white, masculine and feminine. Indeed, each needs the other for definition. I believe in this concept so totally that if I don't see the duality in something, I don't trust my understanding of it yet.

Understanding the principle of duality was a profound guide for me as a young mother, during one of the most challenging periods of my life. I had to confront the wolf, like the last little pig did. Not only was it a guide, but also as I see now, it provided a formative example of putting into practice a principle that I just knew intellectually. It set a pattern for my life to practice the principles and truths in my everyday life, and not let them be an intellectual pursuit alone.

The wolf got into my house. Our son was hit and run over by a car when he was four years old, and was in a critical condition for two weeks. To handle the stress, I divided the time up into two-hour intervals, and would celebrate each time period that he survived. After a couple of days, however, the stress was taking its toll. I asked one of the nurses if there was a spare room I could go and pound on a bed. (This is the technique I used at home when things were too stressful with two pre-school children.) I wasn't mad at anyone in particular, just the situation.

With the pounding, I released a lot of negative energy, and I felt somewhat better. That gave me enough of a release to remember the three little pigs and the eating of the wolf. This was a good "theory," but how could I accept what happened to my precious little boy child? Somehow I knew I had to give up my attachment to him, if he had any chance of living. I had a lot of time to think as I sat there, staring at the "Waiting Room" sign. I remember feeling "at one" with other grieving mothers and thinking how fortunate I was to know at least where my son was.

What would help me "eat the wolf?" And then I remembered the Yin Yang. Would the wholeness of all be a way to help me detach, if I could see the situation as whole and not just negative?

I started searching for the positive of the accident. I didn't tell anyone; they probably would have thought I was delirious. I was driven because I knew that unless I got out of the negativity, I was in no shape to help Matt survive or to see clearly. Then, too, I was in crisis mode and thinking about what other people thought of me was low on my list. I was animalistic, like a mother bear with her cub.

The accident happened in Hollister, California, but after a short time in emergency, he was transferred to a larger hospital in Salinas. I remember when we arrived there, Matt's ambulance had already arrived. At the emergency entrance there was a ramp for the ambulance. Rather than walk around to either end, I climbed up over the ledge, crawling on my hands and knees. I still had my hair in curlers, because we had planned to go out to my husband's high school reunion that night. (Usually, I didn't go out of the house with my hair in curlers. I didn't care about that either.)

During those weeks that Matt was in Intensive Care and critical, I concentrated on the small white dot on the black half side of the Yin Yang, hoping it would lead me to the white side. It took two long weeks to find the white dot and then the white side, enabling me to see the experience as whole. In these written words, this sounds simple, but it was an intense time. While my inner searching was going on, my husband and I took turns at Matt's bedside being strong and loving toward him, projecting healing light. When each of us left his room, we broke down and cried. Perhaps only another parent with a child in a life and death struggle would understand this intensity.

I was able to find some positive which led me to discover the wholeness of the experience. That empowered me to "eat the wolf," to accept Matt's death if need be. It allowed me to release Matt, to say if he were too damaged to live, I would accept his death. I released him into God's hands. (Today, I have a different understanding about who controls death. I believe that the person himself decides, not an outside force. But, nevertheless, I gave up my will.) The profound thing was... Matt didn't start to get better until I released him.

He lived, and today he is a vibrant soul. It was the knowing and believing in the Universal Principle of Duality, the wholeness of all, that allowed me the surrender and detachment that was necessary.

Matt became an unusual kid. He was serious because of his accident. He said he had to decide if he wanted to live at age four. In high school, he studied world religions on his own, and tried to answer some of the "why" and "what" questions for himself. Back then, when Matt got frustrated with not having more than superficial conversations with girls, I tried to explain that girls at that age just wanted to have fun, not talk about the meaning of life.

When he was 17, he told me he wanted to give me the present of eternal life for my birthday. At that time, I said I wasn't sure that I wanted that. (Today, I realize we all have that already, because our spirit never dies.) He told me to write down what I thought was the most important thing, and he would pass it on to his children. It took me about two years to compose the letter.[2] I am writing about that 1986 letter here because the most important thing I wanted to pass on to him was the concept of the duality as seen in the Yin Yang, because it saved him, me, and my marriage during that critical time.

I was able to apply this principle before Matt's accident because I already had an intellectual understanding of the Yin Yang. I had read *The Hiding Place* by Corrie Ten Boom about her personal experience in a Nazi concentration camp. She was interned in a barracks that was infested with fleas, and all the women were bitten. (This situation with fleas seems especially negative to me, since I have an allergic reaction to fleas and dislike the bites so much.) While there, the women wanted to discuss religion and the Bible, which was strictly forbidden. Despite the flea irritation, Ms. Ten Boom accepted the flea situation. She had the faith that fleas were not all negative; there was a positive side, even though she was not sure what it was. Later she found out the reason they were able to have secret religious discussions was that the guards stayed away from her barracks, because the fleas were so bad there. That was a positive to the negative of the fleas.

A friend asked me recently what was the positive I found that enabled me to see Matt's accident as whole. One thing I learned was to live in the present as much as possible. In the next moment, you never know what will happen. Your whole universe can be shattered in the blink of an eye. (That weekend we drove from our home in Berkeley to Hollister, planning to be gone for a weekend. We didn't return home for two weeks.)

I learned that quality of life is as important, if not more, than quantity of life. (Matt gave so much in his life up until that point.) I also gained an appreciation for the complexity and wonder of our physical bodies, and that every drug has both positive and negative effects. (It was explained to us that they were going to have to discontinue one of the drugs they were giving Matt, because it could cause blindness.)

There was a lot of praying going on at that time, and I

clarified for myself what I considered to be most appropriate. I decided that never again would I pray for what I wanted to happen. Since duality exists, it would not be all positive. Besides, how was I to know what is right for another person and what is best in the long run.) My prayers would state my preference, but with the knowledge that I am not in charge of what is best. I would also acknowledge that I would accept whatever would happen and not resist it.

In these last four years, my prayers are more focused on listening, rather than talking. In my quiet times, I am in a state of being, opening my inner eyes and ears for messages. As I move through the day, I have extended my awareness to look and listen for messages sent through the outer world. They come in unexpected ways, from an unhappy person in the line at the grocery store, to the child who is squealing with delight holding his favorite cereal, to finding a parking place, to having a driver next to me become furious at the one in front of him. These are lessons to teach me the positive lessons of compassion, joy, thankfulness, acceptance and non-judgment. I have learned that God teaches me to love in many ways and languages.

My experience with Matt taught me to appreciate the negative because without it, one can't appreciate the positive. The experience gave me depth in understanding myself and others, and a feeling of oneness with all who were undergoing life-and-death crises. During Matt's critical time, a friend gave me a little plaque saying "We can only appreciate the miracle of a sunrise if we have waited in darkness." (Anonymous) I knew that to be true because I had lived it.

I also learned about thankfulness. Our daughter, who is 16 months older than Matt was hit also, but the car only brushed her arm. We were so thankful for that. I also met a mom in the hospital whose son had Spina Bifida. He would never be able to walk because of an opening in his spine. He was an adorable five-year old, scooting around the ward, lying on a skateboard. She turned to me and said, "We are so thankful that he has his mind." She was grateful, in spite of their circumstance. It brought a tear to my eye and taught me a huge lesson -- be thankful no matter what situation you find yourself. It could always be worse.

Swami Sai talks about the necessity and interrelationship of the duality.[3]

> What man has to aspire for today is not happiness. It is not sorrow either (to gain wisdom). In fact, happiness and sorrow are only transitory in nature. Man's duty is to realize Divinity in the unity of happiness and sorrow. Even while you feel elated at the prospect of happiness, you will encounter sorrow. Similarly even while you feel depressed on account of sorrow, happiness will beckon you. Since ancient times, several great sages made efforts to rise above the feelings of happiness and sorrow. They recognized the fact that it was only in times of sorrow that the Divine nature in a human being manifested.... More than happiness, it is sorrow that is helpful to man in several ways. It is only from sorrow, that happiness springs. The main source of happiness in man is sorrow. Just as we welcome happiness, we must welcome sorrow also.

Good/Evil -- Right/Wrong -- Positive/Negative

Here are three pairs of powerful dualities that many people find confusing. I, too, wondered why some people thought something was good and right, while others thought the same thing was evil and wrong. Who is right? Does this mean that good and evil are not objective, not absolute, not black and white? Absolutely. That is why I used the term "perceived" when talking about the opposites earlier. Good and evil are subjective judgments, up to the person's own value system and beliefs as to how to label something. It's decided by one's own value judgments, and what one believes is true. William Shakespeare counsels, "Nothing is evil, lest thinking make it so."

Therefore, this Christmas gift bag makes an appropriate request of Santa:

© HALLMARK LICENSING, INC.

If duality exists, is there something that is only good with no evil, or only evil without a hint of good? No. The Universal Principle of the Yin Yang says there are always the two -- see the small dots in the opposite sides. Not just black or just white; not just evil or just good.

The New Earth, by Eckhart Tolle, presents a story of a man who understood duality and therefore did not judge something as good or evil. He aligned himself with a higher order. This is the story.[4]

> ...of a wise man who won an expensive car in a lottery. His family and friends were very happy for him and came to celebrate. 'Isn't it great!' they said. 'You are so lucky.' The man smiled and said, 'Maybe.' For a few weeks he enjoyed driving the car. Then one day a drunken driver crashed into his new car at an intersection and he ended up in the hospital, with multiple
> injuries. His family and friends came to see him and said, 'That was really unfortunate.' Again the man smiled and said, 'Maybe.' While he was still in the hospital, one night there was a landslide and his house fell into the sea. Again his friends came the next day and said, 'Weren't you lucky to have been here in (the) hospital.' Again he said, 'Maybe.'

Be careful what you wish for; you might get it. Have you seen the downside of your desire? I have fond memories of the TV program "Fantasy Island," which ran from 1978-1984, because it was such a good example of duality. There were stories of visitors to a unique resort island, which could fulfill any fantasy requested. These adventures should be impossible, but this island could accommodate them -- visits to any time period they wanted, meet absolutely anyone they wanted, enact any feat they wanted. The program always showed the people having to face the negative aspect of their dreams.

In one episode, a man wished to be irresistible to all women. He was given a special cologne, but he used too much of it. He found that it was not as positive as he had imagined, having women chase him all the time, and he decided the only woman he really wanted was his fiancée. In another, "Bet A Million," a couple travels to Fantasy Island dreaming of meeting a wealthy investor. They weren't aware that the meeting would be at the Baccarat table with all their assets on the line. They had to risk it all to make their dream come true.

In the Bible, Adam and Eve were banished from the Garden of Eden because they ate the fruit from the Tree of the Knowledge of Good and Evil. Before they tasted the fruit, everything was perfect, good, and unconscious. They did not judge. Then, they ate from the tree, and things changed. They became conscious and judged something as good or evil, so they were banished from "heaven on earth" to reap the consequences of their judgments.

We all are full of those apples from the tree; we all judge to some extent or another. According to Matthew 7:1-2, Jesus said, "Judge not, lest you be judged." This does not mean that we should not evaluate because we have moved into consciousness, but should we condemn another based on our subjective value system? Most of the time we do not see the whole picture. In addition, if we are judgmental people, we not only judge others, we also judge ourselves, which is damaging. Perhaps it was only the Masters (Jesus, Buddha, Lao Tzu, among others) who did not judge at all, and perhaps were seen as enlightened because of that quality. Perhaps they knew that every person is a part of God and to judge another is to judge God. Neale Donald Walsch puts it in these words.[5]

> ...that everything you see, hear, touch, taste, smell, or sense in any way is an aspect of Divinity. It is when you judge it to be something else that it shows up as something else in your life. Therefore, judge not, and neither condemn. For that which you judge, judges you; and that which you condemn will condemn you. Yet that which you see

for what it really is will see you for what you really are. And therein will be found your peace.

In "Sai Inspires," the Swami counsels:[6]

> ...when you turn your mind towards God, who is pervading the entire Universe, the mind will be wholly filled with God, and you won't see the different forms of the objects in the world. But if the mind is directed towards worldly objects, you will fail to see the Divinity that pervades all objects.

Judgment is the cause of wars, nationally and personally -- the other is wrong and I am right. What does "In God We Trust" mean on our currency? What do we trust God to do? Do we trust Him and Her to be on our side, because we are always right, and the other country is always wrong? Is what is good for us, always good for them? Is that our collective thinking? If so, no wonder we go to war.

Why is understanding duality important in daily life? In both positive and negative cases, it gives you a larger perspective of what is true and real. When something positive happens, it helps to be grounded and not be surprised when the drawback shows up. When something negative happens, it helps to resolve the negative: look for the positive, see the wholeness, and be free of the negative. There are common sayings in our culture about the opposites. "When one door closes, another one opens." "Every cloud has a silver lining." It helps one to resolve all that is considered negative and to live in the positive.

This is the stability the three little pigs were looking for, to have their houses stable so that when evil came along, they could withstand it. The story was symbolic, written from the physical perspective. For us, it is a question of emotional stability. I have found that understanding and living this Universal Principle helps me understand myself and others, our thoughts and actions. It helps us to be compassionate and understanding, to love unconditionally.

Beyond the Opposites

The Universe has a bias toward the positive. All that is positive is in the flow with life processes, and is in a level beyond and above the duality of the opposites. Frankly, it is not intelligent to be negative, because the Universe does not support negativity. The negative blocks, stops, and mires down the flow of creativity and progress. Positive is a higher consciousness and continues the evolution of mankind. Quantum physics teaches us that all is a vibration, a wave, a flow of energy. To move beyond the opposites is a movement of energy.

With the Yin Yang principle, the movement is from a singular simplicity (seeing just good <u>or</u> bad) to a duality (good <u>and</u> bad), to a simplicity (good, whole, oneness, beyond the opposites). It is not going back to the Garden of Eden, where there was a perfection in unconsciousness, but forward to a perfection in consciousness. Because of the importance of this higher simplicity, I wrote my son another letter in 2009, explaining the concept of oneness beyond the opposites.[7]

If one sees something simply, it could mean that it is either the start or the finish. How are you to know? Have you seen the complexity of it -- the duality, the opposite, more than one aspect? If so, it is possible that it is the completion. There is a saying -- to return to the beginning and see it for the first time. It is the same, yet entirely different. That "final" simplicity is the beginning of a new simplicity /complexity/ simplicity. That new status is a newer high with newer understanding. There is no beginning and no end as with energy that is never lost, but just changes.

People have said that their elderly parents are acting as if they were children again, reverting back. Yet, the parents have more experience than a child. They are moving forward into the final, more complex simplicity.

Consciousness is elevated in the final simplicity because one is seeing a higher truth -- oneness, which is beyond the opposites. That principle transforms and melds the opposites and leads one to a higher ground where there is stability when forces start to rumble.

Why is this important on a personal basis? In this more complex simplicity, when the wolf is at our door, we can see everything as good, right and perfect. This is a profound consciousness and a key to inner peace. The negative is seen and accepted as learning, and adds great depth and power to one's understanding. Living with a minimum of negative emotions enables one to live in a state of love that includes understanding, compassion, and non-judgment. For those who are comfortable with spirituality, one sees that God/the All is only positive, wishing and supporting all processes in the universe with love. God's gift to us and our gift to ourselves are to understand a larger picture than what seems immediate and on first observance, negative. As Neale Donald Walsch advises, "It's not how many terrible things we have in our lives, but the number of times we call them terrible."

Discoveries of positive aspects in a conflicting situation and its resolution often do not come quickly. In our world where outer gratifications seem more immediate, resolutions of a psychological and spiritual nature often have to be approached with strong intent, belief and patience. Perhaps something or someone (our Higher Self?) is testing, to see if we are really serious before we get an answer?

With escalating neuropathy (sharp pains and over-sensitivity) that I have in my feet, it took me two years to find any positive aspect of what I considered an ongoing negative experience. I knew the experience was whole; I didn't give up. I just kept asking what was the positive, what was the learning? Why did I give myself a foot problem? Most often when I find a positive, I consider it to be much more significant than the negative ever was. And the longer I wrestle with the negative, the positive becomes even more powerful.

What was the answer to my neuropathy question? My dysfunctional feet helped slow me down to allow time for me to write this book. (Indeed, golfing is difficult and acting on stage is out for now.) My medical doctor's response to the answer made me chuckle. She said, "Hurry up and finish the book."

Recently, someone asked me what I loved. I said I loved the beauty of the positive and the power of the negative. I was both surprised and pleased by my answer; I accepted the negative as having an important and positive, not a devastating place in my life. I am willing to sit at as many tables as necessary to eat those wolves that dare enter my home. The reward is that I experience transformations of the negative over and over.

I am convinced that my experiences draw me to a higher consciousness, to my higher self, to the evolution of my soul, to God. What I experience are blessings of great importance, and have more meaning than may be apparent at first. I consider them all positive, even though they might seem negative at first, and/or that I haven't found the positive side of them yet.

Neale Donald Walsch states:[8]

> Your whole life leads you back Home, back to me. Therefore, bless every event, every person, every moment, for each is sacred. Even if you disagree with that event, even if you dislike that person, even if you are not enjoying that moment, all are sacred for Life informs life about life through the process of Life itself, and there is nothing more sacred than Knowing, and then Experiencing, what Life has to tell us about our Selves.

How would our lives be different if we saw that it is possible to move beyond the duality of the Yin Yang, and see every moment as sacred? Is it really possible to live in a state of heaven on earth? Heaven is an attitude and a state of being, not a place. People would find it is a grace, an amazing freedom to be able to live in the positive, the final simplicity, the oneness. It is living with the flow of the Universe, in the love of God, one of those who are in line with the new evolution of the consciousness of mankind.

How would the pigs feel after the destruction of their homes and their brush with the wolf? If they were caught in the good/bad duality, they might be mad, resentful, worried and fearful about the cost of rebuilding, full of blame for that evil wolf that threatened and invaded their homes, their security. Would they ever feel safe in their homes again? They might even extend judgment and blame their neighbors for not coming to help them. Why did God do this to them if he was a loving God?

If they had advanced to the complex simplicity of "perfect," they might consider the experience a positive learning. The pigs would be thankful for the knowledge about the sturdiest material for rebuilding, and for remembering that there is no outer security, only one that comes from within. They might consider some re-decorating with new pictures. They would have been pleased that they were able to think clearly, not caught in fear of the wolf that would have clouded their creative actions. And even more paramount, they would have been thankful that it had not been worse, and that they survived. And what about God? Their experience would affirm and deepen their belief that God was truly loving.

ALL IS ONE

All is One is not a grammatical mistake. All is singular. 1 + 1 = 1.

The concept of Oneness is so important that when put into practice it alone could be the solution to all the problems of the world. Many of our laws protecting what we hold dear would not be needed. If we knew that the physical of the earth was One, we would have true respect and stewardship of the land and its animals. If we knew that as a people we were One, there would be compassion for our fellow man -- no hunger, no pillage, and no wars. If we knew that time and space were One, our lives would be much richer, living in the present and not bound by the future or the past, with no regret, fear, worry, blame, guilt, or resentment. If we knew that all religions were One, we'd no longer be judgmental, close-minded or competitive. We would focus on the highest values together, enriching each other in our quests.

James Cameron, director of *Avatar*, winner of Best Picture, Drama and Best Director at the Golden Globes, Sunday, January 17, 2010 stated:[1]

> "*Avatar* asks us to see that everything is connected, all human beings to each other, and us to the Earth. And if you have to go four and a half light years to another, made-up planet to appreciate this miracle of the world that we have right here, well, you know what, that's the wonder of cinema right there, that's the magic..."

Neale Donald Walsch thoughts on Oneness:[2]

> Everything would change. Everything. Politics would change, economics would change, relationships would change, your ideas about careers and parenting and sexuality and conflict resolution and the purpose of all Life -- everything -- would change.

Bahá'u'lláh, (1817-1892), Founder and prophet of the Bahá'í Faith states:

> So powerful is the light of unity, that it can illuminate the whole earth.

The tenets of Kwanzaa, an African-American holiday, state the power and importance of Universal Principles and Oneness. In *The Complete Kwanzaa, Celebrating Our Cultural Harvest* by Dorothy Winbush Riley, the tenets speak of Universal Laws, which are:[3]

> ...divine creative principles that are timeless truths. We live in a universe of law and order, and there are principles by which all our life's experiences, conditions, and events take place.

Its first principle is Umoja, representing unity and oneness. Practitioners see it as "...the foundation that holds all the other principles."[4] It is seen as primary in the home, the community and the nation. They see the greatest success any person achieves is unity with the universal consciousness through oneness with the Creator.

> From that source we realize that everything in the universe is related -- the earth, the sky, oceans, plants, animals, and humans. We are one related family, and whatever happens to one will eventually happen to us all...we should strive to be in unity and harmony with the universal laws that nothing can destroy.[5]

All Physical is One

The concept that our physical universe is one, connected and interrelated, is a scientific truth that has been accepted in principle for decades. Everything is energy and vibration; it never goes away, it just changes form. Co-winner of the Nobel Prize in physics in 1933, Erwin Schrödinger (1887-1961) said that quantum physics revealed the basic oneness of the universe. For those of us who have not studied quantum physics, the Earth's oneness was not a clear concept until the astronauts went out and looked back at Earth, taking pictures from "out of the box." Then, we could see the reality of what our physical universe has always been. The Earth is one organism.

The naturalist and ecologist know that when one animal goes extinct, it affects the whole planet. The food chain is a complex and structured system. If one species becomes extinct, its predator also will die; as will its predator, setting off a chain reaction. Thus, there are laws protecting even the most "insignificant" living creature that is in limited number, be it the spotted owl, the red-legged frog or the checker spot butterfly. Projects have been stopped or redesigned because of endangered species and their habitats. There is nothing in the physical realm that has a separate relationship from anything else.

The water cycle is an excellent example of a closed physical system, and it is so elementary that even pre-schoolers are exposed to the concept. The School Bus video series has a cute but profound story of the water cycle, animated to catch children's attention. The water energy never goes away. It changes form, but it just keeps going around from ocean to clouds to rain, down into the earth or into rivers back to the ocean. It is why environmentalists are so concerned about polluting our water; it is a closed system. In fun, I often like to ask people if they know that Cleopatra or Napoleon may have once drunk the water that they are drinking right now.

Masaru Emoto's *The Hidden Messages in Water* gives us an unusual insight into physical relationships. The book details Mr. Emoto's studies on water, which show that water responds to vibrations from the written word. Words send off a unique vibration that water senses. When one writes words on a piece of paper, and puts that on a bottle of water, the water reacts to the words. (He shows this by the crystals the water forms after reading the vibrations from the words.)[6]

> Water exposed to "Thank you" formed beautiful hexagonal crystals, but water exposed to the word "Fool" produced crystals similar to the water exposed to heavy-metal music, malformed and fragmented.

Mr. Emoto's research applies to all of us. Our body is seventy percent water. Therefore, it makes a difference what words we use.
> The lesson we can learn from this experiment has to do with the power of words. The vibration of positive words has a beneficial effect on our

bodies and on the world, but the vibration from negative words has the power to destroy.[7]

He continues.[8]

> If you become aware of this, you will no longer be able to speak words of anger to those around you, or blame others for your own mistakes and weaknesses. You have the capacity to change the world within a moment. All you must do is make a simple choice. Are you going to choose a world of love and gratitude, or a tortured world filled with discontent and impoverishment? The answer will depend on your attitude at this very moment.

An excellent example of the physical interrelatedness within the United States and how it affected the whole world was the American financial crisis that broke out October 2008. I was amused by the early talk regarding Main Street businesses, as if they were a separate entity with no relationship to Wall Street at all. It was a shock for some when they saw the huge 770-drop in the Dow on Wall Street, October 2008, after the failure of the first vote on the "bail out" package that was to affect Main Street. The reality was there. No aid to Main Street to help the banks resume lending would restrict business, leading to defaults and unemployment. The inaction by the government regarding Wall Street led to the decline in value of the businesses on Main Street that day.

I was talking with a Canadian citizen about the financial mess as we were watching TV at a resort. Just before the House of Representatives voted on the first proposed "bailout" bill he said, "It doesn't apply to us; we live in Canada." I just smiled and said to him, "The world is one organism." Indeed, the Canadian stocks I held went down.

Financial people knew the world financial system was interrelated, and they watched closely and reported the reaction in the rest of the world as the events took place in the U.S. As the first markets opened in Asia after the vote in Congress, financial eyes strained to see how the international markets were reacting. Those markets reacted almost in lock step. Down.

The fact that "all physical" is one seems innocuous when it doesn't affect one personally. When it does, like interfacing directly with one's livelihood (the lumber industry, the salmon fishery, the baby seals, the rain forest, for instance), there can be great resistance to it. In these cases, we must find other opportunities for those whose livelihood or other actions are damaging the ecosystem, not just ignore that this Universal Principle exists. We must remember Bacon's quote "Man can only gain control over nature by obeying it."[9]

All People Are One

Before we explore issues about other people, we must examine oneness with the most important person -- our self. If that is not established, we do not see clearly, and all our beliefs, thoughts, and actions, no matter how good our intentions, can go awry. One's higher self knows all the Universal Principles and Spiritual Truths about what it is to be and function as a genuine human being -- the highest we were born to be, our birthright.

What are the indications of not being at one with our self? We feel inadequate and separate; we do not realize that we are a creator. We don't understand that we create all that is in our experience. If this is not our knowing, we may blame others or God for circumstances that we really control. We may behave like a victim, yet it is in our hands to change the situation. How often do we blame others or situations for "making us mad," or even give credit for "making us happy." We give away our power that is our birthright, and doing so separates us from the oneness and beauty that is ourselves.

Our reactions to happenings in our past also keep us believing and claiming our separation and lack of oneness. There are many avenues to uncover and heal those wounds -- psychologists, psychiatrists, and psychics. We can do this ourselves, however, as we begin to understand how much we are in control of our lives. John 10:34 (New International Version) reports Jesus said, " 'I have said that you are gods'..." attesting to Jesus' understanding of the degree of our power over ourselves. For some, it is their life path to acknowledge and heal the separation in this lifetime. For others, it is not their time.

We see many needs in the world and wish for a change. How does that happen? It certainly has not happened militarily or legislatively. Change can only be lasting if it starts at the smallest unit, inside you and me. It is bringing about the oneness in ourselves that enables right beliefs and, therefore, right action.

The song, "Man in the Mirror," sung by Michael Jackson:[10]

> ...I'm Starting With The Man In The Mirror
> I'm Asking Him To Change His Ways
> And No Message Could Have Been Any Clearer
> If You Wanna Make The World A Better Place
> (If You Wanna Make The World A Better Place)
> Take a Look at Yourself, And
> Then Make A Change...
>
> As we come to understand our own oneness and
> heal the separation within ourselves, we may be

more at ease feeling at one with others. Intellectually, we may be more comfortable hearing the concept after the candidacy and election of President Barack Obama, where "We are One" was often heard during the campaign. It was popularized on a national scale with "We Are One: Opening Inaugural Celebration at the Lincoln Memorial" in Washington, D.C., on Sunday, January 20, 2009. The impact has been made. Indeed, after the election, I think people in the United States feel closer to those of a different ethnicity. I know I do.

The Elders, Oraibi, of the Arizona Hopi Nation, in response to 911, challenge us with "We Are the Ones We Have Been Waiting For."[11]

> ... At this time in history, we are to take nothing personally. Least of all, ourselves. For the moment that we do, our spiritual growth and journey comes to a halt. The time of the lone wolf is over. Gather yourselves! Banish the word struggle from your attitude and your vocabulary. All that we do now must be done in a sacred manner and in celebration. We are the ones we've been waiting for.

Emotionally, oneness with others may be somewhat tougher to accept than our physical oneness and the oneness of our physical universe. How could I be one with someone who is so difficult to be around, or so different in background and ideology than myself? One has to look deeply into oneself and others to see the similarity. I like to think that we are all in camouflage, different on the outside, but the same on the inside. We are all in disguise. Everyday is Halloween.

On a more serious note, the night when Barack Obama became U.S. president-elect, tears came to my eyes. I realized the importance of an African-American winning that vote of confidence, although he likes to refer to himself as a "world citizen." To have him elected to that most prestigious position in our land, a new paradigm was ushered in. A crack had developed in our camouflage, and people were seeing inside, beyond another's outer skin color.

I was filling out a questionnaire recently where they wanted to know my ethnicity. The heading was Race and the choices were listed to check the appropriate one. I crossed off the word Race and put in ethnicity. We are all of the same race, the human race. Homo sapiens. We are just of different ethnicities.

For Whom The Bell Tolls is a well-known novel by Ernest Hemingway. Whether he got the title from the earlier work by John Donne (1572-1631) is unknown. Donne explores the inter-connectedness of humanity in his passage.[12]

> No man is an island, entire of itself; every man is a piece of the continent, a part of the main. If a clod be washed away by the sea, Europe is the less, as well as if a promontory were, as well as if a manor of thy friend's or of thine own were: any man's death diminishes me, because I am involved in mankind, and therefore never send to know for whom the bells tolls; it tolls for thee.

The Ho'oponopono Hawaii healing system that is used by Dr. Ihaleakala Hew Len of Hawaii is a profound example of the principle of oneness. Joe Vitale's book, *zero limits*, details Dr. Len curing a complete ward of mentally ill patients without ever seeing them. He read each chart and then meditated as he recited, "I love you. I'm sorry. Please forgive me. Thank you." The prayer was directed to God with intent and knowledge that the same illness that was in the mentally ill patient, was also in Dr. Len. He was asking God to forgive the cause in himself. No one knows exactly how this "miracle" happened, but the whole ward was healed.

Did you know that Tiger Woods' predicament has perhaps affected you personally? His marital dilemma may have had an impact on your financial picture.[13]

> Study: Woods' woes cost shareholders $12 billion. ... (Two) UC Davis economists compared returns for Woods' sponsors to those of the total stock market and of each sponsor's closet (sic) competitors, a school news release states... Shareholder value fell 2.3 percent—or about $12 billion.

One doesn't have to own the specific sponsor stocks. The loss would affect the overall S&P, index funds, and retirement pension funds.

Oneness is less evident when one only looks at the outer. It is easy to see how we are all different with different gifts and different ways to share those gifts. Our difference has to do with the outer and the physical -- different appearances, different roles and different jobs. Our outer purposes are different. I tried to teach my children as they were growing up that there is no superiority or inferiority with people. People just have different gifts. Some people are better at certain things than others. Everyone is good at something, and a parent's role is to help discover what that is with each child and to encourage that.

Our inner purpose is where we see the similarity. We all desire to be loved, acknowledged and accepted. We desire to be at one with the higher being that we really are, thereby living in inner peace and thankfulness. We have to move beyond our literal, physical mind that has been conditioned by our past beliefs. Our society worships intellect and the mind. In schools, only things that can be measured by testing are taught. What is taught is product, not process. My husband, a university lecturer and studio instructor, laments that many students do not want to understand the subject matter; they only want to know how to get a good grade. Degrees are important for status. Yet, I'm sure you have experienced what I have -- that a degree is on paper only and has little to do with real knowledge and understanding.

My avocation as a theatre actress has given me insights into seeing my oneness with others. To play a role and be a different person, I have to search to find those attributes in myself. I discovered from over 25 years developing characters that I am everything; I just choose to show certain things, to exhibit those parts of myself with which I want to identify and want others to see.

In Numerology, one's Personality is calculated by adding up the corresponding numbers related to the constants in one's name as it appears on one's birth certificate. Personality is defined as what other people see you to be. Actually, it is what we have decided how we want to be seen – our "mask." We are everything in reality and only decide to show and act on certain sides of ourselves.

The Masters have said that the greatest knowledge one can have is self-knowledge. Lao Tzu stated:[14]

>He who knows others is wise;
>He who knows himself is enlightened.

>Gospel of Thomas: 68, reports that Jesus said:

> ... one who knows everything else but who does not know himself knows nothing.

It is this knowledge of self that leads us to seeing our oneness with others.

The consciousness of oneness is creeping into our society. In March of 2008, Kohl's Department Store came up with a new slogan for the spring. "We're All In This Together." It appeared in television ads and played in the stores over and over on the intercom system. About a year later, the song in a different version was playing again. I'm not so sure that they were expanding the concept to world cooperation, however.

There was a trailer out in 2008 for a new film, THE SHIFT, which is expected to come out in 2010. Even the trailer is amazing, showing people from around the world, singing about unity. More than 140 countries are now represented, viewing the website and donating to the cause. The website www.theshiftmovie.com, states:

> *The Shift* is a transcending movement that stems from an uncompromising longing for cultural reform all across the globe...it can be felt as a fundamental desire throughout humanity for peace, social justice and sustainability...and it is manifesting through a swell of activity at the most grass-roots levels of our society!

(Those working with the film are developing tools to) "...share ideas, understand beliefs and inspire action..." (theshiftmovie.com), and have a Twitter page for up-to-date information. One of the tools is a new spiritual website, "The Great Integral Awakening. Pioneering a New Spiritual Path," sponsored by integralenlightenment.com and Integral Life.[15] They are planning a free online teleseminar series and offer meditations you can download.

Because of the issue of oneness of all, if anyone on the planet is not free, neither am I. Sai Baba states:[16]

> Only when unity is achieved will freedom be meaningful. Without unity, to talk about freedom means only freedom in words and not in real life. Freedom should express itself from the heart. Heart here does not refer to the physical heart. 'Heart' is not related to any particular place, time or individual or a country. Hridayam (heart) refers to that Divine principle which is equally present everywhere, at all times and in all people in every country. It has no form. What is regarded as heart in a human body is a transient thing. The freedom consists in the recognition of that Divinity by knowing which all else is known.

When you know yourself in depth -- positive and negative; physically, mentally, emotionally, spiritually -- and accept it, it leads you to the reality that you are at one with all. This is possibly the reason that Masters of the ages have said that self-knowledge is the most important knowledge you can possess; it leads you to the truth of oneness and compassion for your fellow man. Neale Donald Walsch states:[17]

> You must first see your Self as worthy before you can see another as worthy. You must first see your Self as blessed before you can see another as blessed. You must first know your Self to be holy before you can acknowledge holiness in another.

There can be such an unbelievable outcome to knowing and being this truth. Accepting and feeling at one with all, can lead to incredible understanding, forgiveness, joy, love, compassion and gratitude. It brings about At One Ment (atonement) with God, because God is in all.

When Baba Sai was asked "Why is our approach and attitude to others important?" he responded:[18]

> If you enquire deeply, you can visualize God in every human being and in every material. Any *padartha* (matter) should not be looked upon as mere *padartha*, but considered as *parartha* (essence of Divinity). There is a gulf of difference between *padartha* and *parartha*. Since *padartha* is viewed as mere matter and not Divine, its value is demeaned. You should consider everything as Divine. Every drop of blood in your body is suffused with Divinity. The divine Energy has to be properly utilized by entertaining Divine thoughts.
>
> Jo Dunning,[19] a healer and psychic who holds seminars and Internet workshops, relates that the purpose of all the experiences and learning we encounter is to bring us closer to others, to develop kindness and compassion. And then, all that is left is to serve others.

This principle of Oneness enables me to resolve my own anger. First of all, I accept that it happened. Then, I know that I am totally responsible for my own emotions. It has nothing to do with the outer circumstances, and no one has made me feel anything. Therefore, I can just change my perspective and be free of the anger. Oneness is key because it enables a faster movement to resolution. I know I am at one with that person and have the capacity for that negative also. This knowledge enables me to change my attitude from anger to forgiveness and compassion.

Oneness is a lesson of the third house of the little pigs, where the picture on the wall was the pig surrounded by family and others. The highest relationship with our family, be it our generational family or our whole earth family, is one of service. With a focus on giving and accepting vs. taking and expecting, a new evolution of our species would be born, the hope for our world.

Time and Space Are One

This topic is revolutionary. It introduces a completely new way of thinking that is more than psychological; it is based in science. We are hearing more and more from metaphysics and quantum physics about the dimensions of time and space. The old thinking of linear time, where it is understood only as a straight line of before and after, is being reviewed. People are urged to consider time as interdimensional. Interdimensional is a new concept in some dictionaries. Humorously, the spell check in my Word program keeps urging me to change the word to "one-dimensional."

One way to understand "interdimensional" is instead of viewing time as a straight line, envision it as building with three stories and one footprint. The past would be the first story, the present would be the middle, and the future would be the top story. Even this explanation is linear; interdimensionally it would be similar to a helix, all intertwining and mixing. The focus would be in the "now" where the past, present and future are all one. A further refinement would be to see all the stories collapsing into one symbol and within it would be the helix structure.

Here is a diagram approximating the difference between linear time and quantum time.

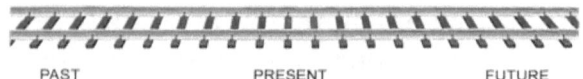

Why does this intellectual concept matter to our daily living?

About 14 years ago, I tested the concept that past, present, and future were stacked on each other. Could I really access the past? I did. I cured myself of a disease called fibromyalgia I'd had for over 15 years. The process I used is called Quantum Healing learned from Kryon of Magnetic Service, an entity that can be accessed in meditation by some. He said because time is stacked and not linear, we could take ourselves back in time before we had the disease. First of all, I handled the disease psychologically. I thought about and gave up any benefit I was getting from the disease ... sympathy and being less useful around the house. Then I concentrated on taking myself back in time. Within a few minutes, I could move my joints with no pain. I could sit with no pain. I was amazed. People have asked me how I did that and I said it took belief and focus.

Another application, wishing for something one doesn't have now, but hopes for in the future, is an error in perception in interdimensional terms. This misconception is why some people have trouble working with The Law of Attraction, which was popularized by the DVD, *The Secret*, and the work of channel Esther Hicks. This concept states that when you desire something you don't have, all you have to do is imagine it, and you will receive it. However in interdimensional terms, there is no past, present or future. All is one, the Now. Out-of-the-box thinking and foreign to our linear minds, interdimensional is seeing that one already has it, because the past, present and future are one. Some who have approached their desires as already accomplished have found this to be true. I would encourage you to experiment with this concept yourself. The Universe works in "strange" ways according to our conditioned thinking.

Neale Donald Walsh states:[20]

> The grandest teaching of Christ was not that you shall have everlasting life -- but that you do; not that you shall have brotherhood in God, but that you do; not that you shall have whatever you request, but that you do.

In the movie *What the BLEEP do we Know...?*, they state that if you can't believe it, you won't see it. I have experienced that many times. When I was pregnant with my first child, I'd look around and it seemed as though "every woman" was pregnant. I just had not noticed the pregnant women before. Many times after learning something new, I have seen it again and again in different contexts. Or when I meet someone new, I consistently run into him or her again soon after. It shows how important our consciousness is. Two applicable quotes are: "When you change the way you look at things, the things you look at change." (Dr. Wayne Dyer) "If we don't like what's happening to us in the world, all we have to do is change our consciousness -- and the world out there changes for us!" (Lester Levenson, *Keys to the Ultimate Freedom*, 1993)

Another aspect of the Law of Attraction is more subtle, but as powerful. When one desires something, the nature of your emotion about it will affect your result. The emotion is either love based or fear based. The response that returns is from a higher power (be it your higher self, God or the All), which only supports the positive because it, itself, is positive. Therefore, if you wish for something out of fear, the outcome you desire will be much less likely. If on the other had it comes from love, you are in vibration with that higher positive and the likelihood will be more likely. For example, you need a new job because you need more money. From a fear base, you are afraid of something that might happen if you don't get one. From a love base, you want to provide support for others in some way. It is a fine distinction, but an important one.

It is postulated by Kryon of Magnetic Service (a group of non-physical beings channeled by Lee Carroll) that in this age if we are in a high vibration, since the past and present are one, we can go back into our former lives and pick up attributes that we wish. He admits that this is an advanced teaching and probably unbelievable by most. I am experimenting with this in writing this book.

If past, present and future are one, what is a "past" life? It is a misnomer. The past is with us, but in another dimension. The evidence of this explains some unusual instances we may experience. It is the cause of déjà vu. It is closer to us than we think. Perhaps the reason that child prodigies advance faster than normal is because they are not starting from a clean slate, but picked up talents and knowledge from a previous life.

Oneness gives insight into various phobias. If not traceable to an experience in their current lifetime, the instance possibly was stored ('cell memory') in a previous lifetime and then activated by the current one. Often the phobia may not be seen until the age when the experience occurred in a previous life. Sometimes the knowledge alone of the true origin may heal the phobia/fear.

Some say that birthmarks are evidences of traumas from a past life. I have an acquaintance who has a round birthmark near his spine on his back. Indeed, sometimes he acts as if he was stabbed in the back.

Kryon of Magnetic Service has said that those who are autistic have problems because they are not linear thinkers in our linear world. What if interdimensionally they are at a higher level, and we are the linear, challenged ones? An interesting thought.

The oneness of time and space is foreign to our linear trained mind. It is against almost everything we have been taught in school. It is the evolution of our species to begin to think interdimensionally. As you think about physically traveling to new places, you might want to include psychic travel (as we do in our dreams) and think about how the past, present, and future play out as One for you.

How do the past, present, and future play out as one for you?

All Religions Are One

Throughout the ages, many of the conflicts we have had with one another were waged in the name of religion -- the Inquisition, the Israeli wars, the Shiites and the Sunnis, Ireland, China and Tibet. It's as old as Cain and Able and continues to this day. Rather than leading us to love our fellow man, organized religions' dogma and intolerance have engendered thoughts of superiority and inferiority, separation, fear, hatred, torture, and killing.

There is an Ojibwa Indian saying, "No tree has branches so foolish as to fight amongst themselves." Bahá'u'lláh also uses the analogy of the tree.[21] "The tabernacle of unity hath been raised; regard ye not one another as strangers. Ye are the fruits of one tree, and the leaves of one branch."

What has gone wrong? In a humorous way, this is the way it is.

NON SEQUITUR © 2007 Wiley Miller
Dist. By UNIVERSAL PRESS SYNDICATE.
Reprinted with permission. All rights reserved.

There are mandalas showing various religions, all with equal emphasis, not one doctrine being superior to another.

Unitarian Universalist

The Creative Initiative Foundation, 1980s

Amara Wahaba Karuna. Karunaarts.com

Newlifeparadigm.com

I have included quotes from Sai Baba in this book because I admire his holistic view. July 4, 1968, he said:[22]

> I have come to light the lamp of Love in your hearts, to see that it shines day by day with added luster. I have not come on behalf of any exclusive religion. I have not come on a mission of publicity for a sect or creed or cause, nor have I come to collect followers for a doctrine. I have no plan to attract disciplines or devotees into my fold or any fold. I have come to tell you of this unitary faith, this spiritual principle, this path of Love, this virtue of Love, this duty of Love, this obligation of Love.

I saw this bumper sticker on a car. The message of Oneness is starting to appear even if the concept is not widely accepted. I was able to Google it and order some from the website *stampandshout.com*.

Kryon of Magnetic Service sees the acceptance of others and their paths in a non-judgmental way.[23]

> Blessed are the human beings who search for Home in their own way, in a building of their own choice, with a priest of their choice, in any way that makes their heart feel the love of God in their way, for they will have light in their heart and have a better life for it.

In the Bible, John 14:2, Jesus is quoted: "In my Father's house are many mansions; if it were not so, I would have told you."

I envision each religion having a spoke on a wheel. A wagon wheel is a good image because the hub of the wheel is important.

Elementary in understanding, we are on a spoke with our own religion, near the outside rim edge. We see a great distance between our spoke and those on each side. As understanding becomes deeper, we move toward the center on our spoke. The separations from the nearby spokes are becoming smaller and smaller; more similarities are seen. When we get to the center of the wheel, the hub, we see that all religions are really saying the same thing. It is the home of God, and one is with God/the All. Neale Donald Walsch calls this re-membering, when one again becomes conscious, in the membership of God.

There is no doctrine in the center, no rules, no place to come to or report to. You don't have to join anything because you already have. You are a piece of God, in the family of spirit. You communicate directly with God with no intermediary. It is the place of Oneness.

If we are militant about our beliefs, thinking it is the only way, and are judgmental about another's, that indicates that we have not entered into a deeper understanding and the essence of our own religion.

What do people living in the hub of the wheel look like? It is not difficult to spot them, though they are few. You can tell by their thoughts and actions. They are free of judgment, of prejudice, of negativities such as hate, worry, blame, fear, regret, and non-forgiveness. They have great understanding, love and compassion for all people. They are not tossed around by the outer world. They have stable natures and live with inner peace, no matter what happens. When my kids were young, I often said I wished to have inner peace in the midst of chaos. It took many years to even begin to see the road to that awareness.

The hub is rich because each religion gives jewels to it in the form of principles. There are a thousand different religions on the Earth, but some of the predominant ones, are as follows:

The Bahá'í faith focuses on the principle of oneness -- one God, one human race, and the different religions being evolutions of God's will and purpose for humanity. Followers believe the time has come for all peoples to unite into a peaceful and integrated society.

Buddhism's Eight-Fold Path symbolizes right views, aims, speech, conduct, living, effort, mindfulness and meditation. When followed with sincerity and discipline, these paths lead to enlightenment.

Christianity believes that God loves all. It points to the underlying oneness and interrelationship of all people -- loving thy neighbor as thyself, the Golden Rule of doing unto others as you would have them do unto you, and judge not, lest you be judged.

Confucianism focuses on ethical teachings, the highest of which is the oneness of all people -- Jen: benevolence, humaneness towards others.

Gnosticism believes in the Oneness of all and provides a guide to help determine what is true. It emphasizes that one must trust one's highest self/one's soul/God within, and asks us to focus on our own experience, not just believe someone else's.

In Hinduism, non-violence and respect for all life are practiced; they see all are a part of God.

Humanism celebrates the best in human attributes, leading to the spirit of enlightenment, which is to be used for the good of all.

The crescent moon of Islam represents the lunar calendar, while the star represents Allah, the divine. Sufism, the more mystical path of Islam, emphasizes the truth found in all religions.

Jainism emphasizes harmlessness to all and focuses on "Three Jewels:" right faith (clear sight), right knowledge (aka, Universal Principles and Spiritual Truths), and right conduct (action based on right faith and right knowledge).

Jorastrianism/Zoroastrianism focuses on the dualities in life: truth and falsehood; and the "Destructive Principle" and the "Bounteous Principle."

In Judaism, a basic belief is that all things were designed to have meaning and purpose, as part of a divine order of one creator of everything.

The Native American spirit reminds us that all creatures are our brothers and sisters, and to honor the spirits and sacred energy in all life forms.

Sikhism's main teachings emphasize God realization, the importance of having a teacher for guidance and instruction, and the importance of detachment from physical matters.

Shintoism morality is based on what is beneficial to the group and emphasizes right practice, sensibility, and attitude.

In Taoism, the Yin Yang symbolizes balance and harmony. It is a symbol of oneness and suggests that those who understand duality and choose to live beyond it, will have lives of wholeness and compassion.

The Unitarian Universalist philosophy embodies We Are One, welcoming all human kind, believing that the diversity leads to beauty, strength, courage, and a respect for the independence of all existence.

The earth-centered religion of Wicca emphasizes the importance of protecting the ecology and resources of our planet.

"Sai Inspires" calls the peacefulness of the hub, Bliss.[24]

> Truly speaking, it is not difficult to know what the basis of life is, and what should be the goal of life. Bliss should be the goal, and one must seek it in all earnestness. The human body is temporary; the pleasure that it can give also is fleeting. Therefore,

one must seek that which is permanent, that is to say, God, or what is the same thing. Bliss. It is meaningless to seek this Bliss by way of instruments that are impermanent. The body can give only bodily pleasure, and the mind can at best give only mental satisfaction. But these do not represent Bliss.

No matter what religious doctrine we follow, if our being is not peaceful inwardly and toward others, we have not understood and experienced the true essence of our religion. In the hub, all is One, because there is great understanding and compassion. With compassion, one sees beyond outer, superficial things that seem to separate us. It is an understanding of "There but by the Grace of God, go I."[25] Living in the hub is true inner peace, the "peace of God that passeth all understanding."[26] One understands the warning "Never criticize a man until you walk a mile in his moccasins." (Native American adage)

The universe urges us to live in the "hub of the wheel" and to acknowledge the jewels of all religions. Much depth in beauty and richness resides there. The Law of Allowing from the Abraham-Hicks writings challenges us to welcome and learn from the variety of disciplines. They advise us that to accept them all is to accept all of God, and one's self. To deny any of them is to deny a part of God and one's self.

This Principle of Oneness is the key to "heaven on Earth" because it generates the feeling of love, overcoming separation. Most people wish for this outcome (whether they call it that or not), but it does not happen by wishing or by chance. In *The Journey Home, a Kryon Parable (The Story of Michael Thomas and the Seven Angels)* channeled by Lee Carroll, the process is detailed for how one can experience heaven without dying, because heaven on earth is a state of being, not a place. A key to heaven or hell for our world and ourselves is to examine our beliefs to see what aligns with the Universal Principle of Oneness, and to see how we are working with it or against it.

The three little pigs in their final act, acted as one in the internalization of the evil wolf. They ate for the benefit of all. Perhaps they hoped that their unified act would demonstrate what is needed, so that we might understand and manifest the principle of oneness.

WE ARE SPIRITUAL BEINGS

What does spiritual mean? The dictionary defines it as "concerning itself with matters of the spirit, regarding humankind's ultimate nature and meaning." These include concepts such as who am I? What is life really about? What gives life meaning? What is the nature of God, and what is our true relationship with God? These are questions around which our deepest longings and desires are centered.

Most talk about spirituality in intellectual terms, similar to that above. Recently, I shared with someone what I liked most about spirituality was that it is so practical. The person looked at me with a puzzled look. Often people talk about spirituality in vague terms. When I was first learning about spirituality, I was puzzled too, and the book *There is a Spiritual Solution to Every Problem* by Dr. Wayne Dyer caught my attention. How could spiritually be practical? It's so otherworldly. Isn't it?

Neale Donald Walsch explains the relevance of spirituality:[1]

> The problem facing the world today is a spiritual problem. Your ideas about spirituality

are killing you. You keep trying to solve the world's problem as if it was a political problem, or an economic problem, or even a military problem, and it is none of these. It is a spiritual problem. And that is the one problem human beings don't seem to know how to solve.

Perhaps we don't know how to solve it, because we don't understand spirituality. Spirituality holds the key to resolving the negative emotions we encounter everyday, such as blame, guilt, worry, depression and fear, which are the causes of the chaos we see in the world.

Most people equate spirituality with religion, but they are not the same. Religions provide answers to the "who, what, why" questions, and require that you believe their interpretation. Each religion has its own set of directions and tells us what God is and what He wants of us. Spiritualism does not have rules and regulations, and does not require us to believe anything. It asks us to be aware of our own experience; that is our authority. We are not to be guided by what someone else tells us. Religion is an institution, and spiritualism is an experience.

Many religions focus on their own prophets instead of God. They look at the tree and marvel, often worship the tree, because of the way it moves in the wind. They do not realize that the tree is not moving by itself. The tree is still without the catalyst of the wind. The wind is the power, not the tree. God is the power, not the prophet. The prophet has enabled God to work through him or her.

Recently, a friend asked me what is spiritual? I said everything is spiritual, because spirituality is an attitude about life. Everything matters and the least little thing may be important. What defines something is the feeling that you bring to it. Depending on the person, life can be meaningful and spiritual, or meaningless.

Spiritualism leads us to understand that God is indescribable. If anyone tells you that they know what God is, they don't, for God is beyond our knowledge and words. God is in the physical and the spaces that exist in the physical. We have something in common with a chair because God is in us, and in the chair, alike. This is a reason that Spiritual Masters have great respect for everything. Everything and everyone is a part of God.

God has no favorite religion and does not ask us to do things – to go to church or temple or the mosque, or other holy place, because God can be found everywhere. We don't need to develop a relationship with God because we already have one. We don't even need to pray to God about what is happening in our lives because He/She already knows that.

When the false beliefs of our inadequacy and the nature of our world are healed within ourselves, the spiritualist realizes his/her co-creative power. We realize that God does not do things for us, or to us. Therefore, we cannot blame God for anything that happens. It is revolutionary (perhaps evolutionary might be a better word) to believe that God is not the primary actor in the universe. People are the actors on the stage. God has an input with the script but, without people, there is no play. Then too, it is difficult to separate people from God, because all is one; people are a part of God, and God is a part of people.

Bahaman Sri Sathya Sai Baba states:[2]

> The word "Adhyatmic" or spiritual is often used by aspirants and preceptors. What exactly is implied when this word is used? Is Bhajan or congregational prayer Adhyatmic? Or, does it

involve religious rituals and ceremonies? Or, does it involve Japa and Dhyana? (Repetition of Names of the Lord and Meditation)? Or does it extend to pilgrimages to holy places? No, No! These are merely beneficial acts. Adhyatmic in its real sense is related to two progressive achievements or at least sincere attempts towards those two achievements -- Elimination of the animal traits still clinging to human beings and unification with the Divine.

So how do we come to understand and unite with the Divine? The Eastern religions give us the best clue. Be still. Quiet the mind. Meditate. Open up to the silence. Show your Higher Self/God/the higher dimensions that you realize what occupies your mind most of the time is less important. When still, channeled knowledge is passed from non-physical beings on the Other Side to those here on Earth who have a high vibration and a clear channel to hear.

Here are a few channelers and some are quoted in this book -- Edgar Cayce, Neale Donald Walsch, Jane Roberts (channeling Seth), Esther Hicks (channeling Abraham), Lee Carroll (channeling Kryon), Jach Pursel (channeling Lazaris), April Crawford (channeling Veronica), Sri Ram Kaa and Kira Raa (channeling Archangels), Shondra -- Rose of Light, Tom Kenyon (channeling Mary Magdalen, the Hathors, and various angels), Gary Renard (channeling Arten and Pursah), Evanne Jordan (channeling Ish), Summer Bacon (channeling Dr. James Peebles), and Sylvia Browne (channeling Francine and Raheim).

Spiritualists know that higher consciousness is relayed in a disguised form, so that only those who are ready to benefit will understand. They learn about God from everywhere and everything. God talks to us in many ways, and you have to be alert for the unseen. In addition, spiritualists know that attitudes and feelings are spiritual issues. It's more than what you do, but why you do it, and how you feel about it. It is a function of the right side of our brain that handles feelings.

We are all on a spiritual path whether we are aware of it or not. That is why we came to Earth, to learn (actually remember) who we really are (spiritual beings), and to learn how to resolve the negativity we experience, and transform it into the various expressions of love. We get sidetracked however, and instead think that the car, the job, the "soul mate," the house will fill that deeper need.

Some of these sidetracks are quite humorous. One is called the *Attractor Genie* (The Law of Attraction software). According to their website, attractorgenie.com, by using their software, which is only $97:

> ALL your limiting money beliefs will be erased - AUTOMATICALLY
> Your ability to be broke will vanish - AUTOMATICALLY
> Money will never again be a problem - AUTOMATICALLY
> You will end procrastination forever - AUTOMATICALLY
> You will live the life of your dreams – on your terms – starting today.
> And so much more...

Then, too, there is the "Wash Away Your Sins," liquid soap, breath spray, soap, and towelettes from Blue Q (www.blueq.com). They also carry the "Looking Good For Jesus" line.

Anyone advanced on the true spiritual path is caught up less with the outer, and is most interested in developing a nature that is positive, thankful, peaceful, and devoid of negativity in any form -- judgment, hate, blame, fear, non-forgiveness, worry, unrest. That state is held regardless of what is happening to the person or in the world. Our thoughts, attitudes and actions are the evidence of our spirituality, not by what religion we belong to or profess to believe. The Masters experienced this positive state in totality. For others, traveling a spiritual path is a real workout. We have to catch ourselves in the negativity and change it right away. It is a discipline, as if we were Olympic athletes training for a physical sport.

One religion (relatively unknown) gives a unique perspective on who we are and why we are here. Because it is quite unknown and because it has some useful principles for resolving negativity, I will discuss it here.

Gnosticism is a spoke on the wheel, along with the others. (It is not Agnostic, those who doubt God exists.) Gnosticism asks us to focus on our own experience, rather than just having faith in someone else's. Does something make sense to you? Rely on your higher self for validation, the God within. Gnosticism states that we are a much higher level than "human," basing our thoughts and actions totally on the physical plane. Gnosticism, a religion in Jesus' time, means "gnosis" (knowledge or wisdom). Experience is most important, not dogma. Gnosis was influential until the 4th century, when the newly founded Christian Church violently suppressed it as "heresy."

Gnosticism states that we are spiritual beings and have come into this lifetime to learn lessons to further perfect our souls. "We are not human beings having a spiritual experience. We are spiritual beings having a human experience." (Teilhard de Chardin, French geologist, priest, philosopher and mystic, 1881-1955)

Those who follow Gnosticism believe that while on the Other Side before we were born, we planned certain lessons for ourselves to experience, to further perfect our souls and to wake up to who we really are -- divine, spiritual beings. We are a part of God, and our purpose is to love, no matter the circumstance. That we planned our experiences (both "good" and "bad") can be a life-changing concept. If one believes this, it substantially reduces the amount of negativity one experiences in life. There is no blame or guilt; we planned it for ourselves as a lesson.

We are active participants, and do not take a passive position that God or someone else did something to us. All we have to blame, if we want to, is ourselves. Blame, in itself, is thinking something is negative, not accepting that there is a positive experience for us to benefit from. (Remembering wholeness, a positive comes with everything we view as negative.) Knowing and living this concept makes it possible for a person to live in inner peace during times that others might find very stressful.

Gnosticism also teaches that there are no accidents or coincidences. An "accident" is a lesson we had planned for ourselves. If it results in one's death, the person had decided that his or her mission this lifetime was over. That is hard to fathom, especially with a young, vibrant person. But it is up to that person to decide for himself. Perhaps the person felt his mission in life was complete. Perhaps he was playing a role to help others with their soul's perfection in terms of judgment or compassion. Perhaps for some reason, he wanted to relocate (through reincarnation) to a different time and place.

If we planned the circumstance, the issue of forgiveness is moot. There is nothing to forgive, because no one harmed us. We did it to ourselves to learn from. If one does not believe this and continues to blame, one is only hurting one's self.

Naomi Judd advises: "Know forgiveness, know peace. No forgiveness, no peace."

The parable of "The Little Soul and the Sun" tells of one soul helping another with forgiveness.[3]

> "You may choose to be any Part of God you wish to be," I (God) said to the Little Soul. "You are Absolute Divinity, experiencing Itself. What Aspect of Divinity do you now wish to experience as You?"… "…I choose Forgiveness. I want to experience my Self as that Aspect of God called Complete Forgiveness."

The story says that there was a challenge because everyone was perfect in Heaven so there was no one to forgive. Then a Friendly Soul stepped forward and said that he would come into the Little Soul's next physical lifetime and do something for the Little Soul to forgive. When the Little Soul asked the Friendly Soul why he would want to do such a thing, the Friendly Soul said because I love you and because you have done it for me. He continued:

> "Of course. Don't you remember? We've been All Of It, you and I. We've been the Up and Down of it, and the Left and the Right of it. We've been the Here and the There of it, and the Now and the Then of it. We've been the Big and the small of it, the Male and the Female of it, the Good and the Bad of it. …"

> The Friendly Soul explained that those people who require forgiveness are "God's Special Angels, and these conditions God's Gifts." The Friendly Soul asked for just one thing in return.

> "In the moment that I strike you and smite you," said the Friendly Soul, "in the moment that I do the worst to you that you could every imagine -- in that self-same moment...remember Who I Really Am."

Think for a moment of a circumstance where you might be having a problem of some kind with another person. What if they are a Friendly Soul? What if we could think of our time here on Earth merely as play -- playing with Friendly Souls. Then too, what if we are just playing with different energies. For instance, if I think of a situation as an energy of rejection rather than a rejection from the person, the negativity of the situation is lessened, and it is easier to view the situation as a lesson and the person as "friendly."

Planning one's life before being born is a concept also supported by Numerology, a study originated by Pythagoras, where letters have an energy and have corresponding numbers linked to them. The numbers are reduced to one and sometimes two digits, which have corresponding meanings. The theory behind Numerology is that while on the Other Side, before coming into this lifetime, we planned what kind of a person we wanted to be, and what road we wanted to walk, all to further perfect our souls. In working with my own numbers and the profiles of more than 80 others, most people find they are uncannily accurate. However, some discover they may not be adhering to the path that they had planned.

There are nine Expression/Destiny numbers, corresponding to 1-9, plus three, main Master Numbers. This indicates of the type of person we wanted to be. This is determined by our name as it appears exactly on our birth certificate. Numerology states that our parents did not name us; we infused the name we wanted into their minds. A "mistake" here with the "wrong" name or misspelled name on the birth certificate is not really a mistake, according to Numerology, it is really what you planned.

There are nine Life Paths, derived from our date of birth, corresponding to the numbers 1-9, plus three main Master Numbers. One path is not better than another. We decided this is the path we wanted to travel this lifetime.

We are all playing the game of life, but with different Life Path and Expression adaptations on different awareness levels. Because we all have unique numbers, we must rely on our own experiences. We need to walk and discover our own path, not someone else's.

Neale Donald Walsch explains in "I Believe God Wants you to Know" that[4]

> ...words may help you understand something, but experience allows you to know.

Spiritualists say that we choose different adventures for each of our lives because we want to experience it all. Therefore, some current lives are more demanding than others. For some, this life is a "vacation," if we have had an especially difficult experience in our previous life.

It is folly to compare your self with another. You want to discover and advance on your own path. To compare and experience jealousy of another person's path is a detour from your own highest destiny. It would be like changing trains without knowing the destination of the other train. Besides, if you were due a vacation this time, you wouldn't want to miss it, would you?

A more advanced (interdimensional) concept needs to be mentioned concerning Numerology, as it relates to time and space. We are in our present life and present Numerology

Profile, but are we not also all our "past" lives with their profiles? (Again, it is imaging we are similar to a building with many floors and one footprint.) We are so much more than we can ever know.

Eckhart Tolle in *The New Earth*, simplifies our pure nature even beyond being spiritual beings. We are "Beings." This is the purest essence because there is no outer label. Tolle says to add any label is to err. It is also the same with God. God is beyond labels, beyond understanding, beyond all. To label or identify in any way is to diminish. In that way, as in many, we are the same as God.

We may or may not realize we are spiritual beings and on a spiritual path in this lifetime. However, we are perfect, following our own path and doing exactly what we came here to do. Here again is Divine Chaos. We may consider our situation "chaos," while our higher self considers it "divine." Our birthright is to evolve to the highest we can become, to resolve our inner separation and realize our oneness with self, God and all. It is a blessing and hope for us all, and the only hope for the planet.

What would the three little pigs think of humans being spiritual, rather than just human? For a pig to imagine that the spiritual exists is an extreme stretch, since their thoughts and actions are limited by their physical genetic code. As you will see in the next chapter, as Homo sapiens we have 11 levels higher than the physical in our genetic code. We have to ask ourselves if we want to limit ourselves to a physical preoccupation, similar to animals. We have an amazing advantage, a destiny beyond words, and a responsibility as co-creators.

THE UNSEEN CONTROLS THE SEEN

Are you aware that the unseen controls you? This has nothing to do with science fiction.

The unseen are non-physical; they cannot be seen with our physical senses of sight or touch. They are energies -- feelings, emotions, ideas, beliefs, concepts, principles, and attitudes. The seen are what we see in the physical world around us -- people, houses, cars, furniture, trees, and mountains.

The seen is elementary because it is visible; the unseen is elusive because it requires more attention, a higher level of consciousness. "Some of the most beautiful things in life cannot be seen or touched -- they are felt with the Heart." (Helen Keller, on a plaque by L. Voskuil-Dutter)

Kryon of Magnetic Service (as channeled by Lee Carroll) states that within our DNA are 12 levels and only one of them (the physical) is seen and can be documented. He says that we use all of our brain, but do not use our entire DNA. The remaining 11 levels have interdimensional capacities that remain unexplored.[1]

People value, celebrate and love the seen -- the houses, the cars, designer clothes, jewelry, travel and all that money will bring. We value how we look and desire youthfulness; think of the number of products that support skin and hair care alone. We, women, adorn ourselves with fancy clothes, necklaces, bracelets, rings, and take care of our nails with manicures and pedicures.

In addition, we have a love/hate relationship with our bodies. When I catch myself with a negative attitude, I remind myself what is good about my body, and how the body part in question could always be worse. Just being thankful that it works at all (especially at my age) with all its complexity is sobering. It is normal to take our bodies for granted; and often we don't really appreciate them until some part goes wrong. As Michael Beckwith says, "The enlightened give thanks for what most people take for granted."

Look to the unseen again for clues about your physical body. Veronica, non-physical being channeled by April Crawford, states:[2]

> Your physical being is but a product of your soul.
> To change what is externally created one must
> reach to the inner core of the self to find peace and
> clarity.

Indeed, psychologists agree that the outer manifestations of being overweight or having clutter challenges must be changed from the inner; one cannot just fix the outer. These issues have deep-seeded psychological causes. Why do we feel we have to eat to comfort ourselves? Comfort ourselves, because of what? Why do we hoard and focus on things? What need is being covered up? What is really missing in our lives?

Not only do we clamor after it, most people identify with the physical. I chuckled recently when I was behind a "sexy," new Lexus sports car whose license plate read CMYCAR. Did he
identify with his car or not? Is he more than his car? Are those who have a car like his better than those who don't? Attachment to the physical, like the little pig who won a strength contest, causes much unhappiness and lack of fulfillment in our world. If someone doesn't have it and someone else does, they fight to get it. It's one the causes of war. If the issue of the car doesn't strike you, think oil.

Manly P. Hall in *The Secret Teachings of All Ages* states:[3]

> Ignorant of the cause of life, ignorant of the purpose of life, ignorant of what lies beyond the mystery of death, yet possessing within himself the answer to it all, man is willing to sacrifice the beautiful, the true, and the good within and without upon the blood-stained altar of worldly ambition. The world of philosophy -- that beautiful garden of thought wherein the sages dwell in the bond of fraternity -- fades from view. In its place rises an empire of stone, steel, smoke, and hate -- a world in which millions of creatures potentially human scurry to and fro in the desperate effort to exist and at the same time maintain the vast institution which they have erected and which, like some mighty, juggernaut, is rumbling inevitably towards an unknown end. In this physical empire, which man erects in the vain belief that he can outshine the kingdom of the celestials, everything is changed to stone. Fascinated by the glitter of gain, man gazes at the Medusa-like face of greed and stands petrified....
> Religion, too, has become materialistic: the beauty and

> dignity of faith is measured by huge piles of masonry, by tracts of real estate, or by the balance sheet.

In the Bible, Matthew 19:24 states, "It is easier for a camel to go through the eye of a needle, than for a rich man to enter into the kingdom of God." Scholars disagree on the origin of this saying, however the common understanding is that you have to unload your camel to get through the narrow gates of the cities. The verse pertains to the unseen and not the seen; this does not mean that you have to give away your worldly possessions. The symbology is that we have to unload ourselves from the beliefs about who we think we are, in order to live in inner peace. We are not anything like what others see on our outside -- our possessions and our job titles. When we identify with outer titles and jobs -- mother, father, lawyer, dentist, secretary, doctor, architect, teacher -- we give them value judgments. Does that mean that the person with the higher status job or title has a higher value as a person?

In my early 50s, I entered a major depression, because I felt I was a nobody. I now refer to this as my desert period. Many of my friends had advanced degrees, "valued" professions, titles and status. I did not consider myself "successful." I was not a medical doctor, a lawyer, an architect, or some other highly valued title. I allowed myself to be brainwashed that the job title was what made a person of value. I was depressed, thinking that the outer role was what was important in life. I was a college graduate and a licensed Medical Laboratory Technologist, but stopped working when the family came along. I told my medical doctor about feeling depressed and not having meaning in my life because I was not a high-level professional. She said it certainly didn't come from being a medical doctor. That shocked me.

> ...We must ask ourselves: "What am I NOT?" I'm not my house, not my car, not my relationships.

> We are NO THING. Once we realize this, it will then be pretty easy to go through the eye of a needle.[4]

I first got a glimpse of the unseen, the deeper part of myself, when I was at a seminar in the 1990s. We did an exercise in pairs in which the other person asked you over and over, "Who are you?" I quickly went through all my titles and roles and then...I went into another kind of dimension. I left my body and became some kind of pure awareness. I moved to just outside Earth, encircled it and embraced it. It was like I was only consciousness. That is what I called it at the time. I was truly euphoric, and remained in that state for about a week. I didn't know what happened to me, but now I consider it my first actual experience of my spirit, my true and deepest self. I have had other experiences of my true self more recently. Words cannot explain the magnificence of them.

My desert period ended in my mid-50s, when I reentered a spiritual quest. The impetus came from a strange question from the leader of a spiritual seminar that I was attending. She asked if I felt at home on Earth. I said that I did. As we talked, she told me that she felt my last lifetime was on a planet different than Earth. That so intrigued me, I started my spiritual searching again. Now I realize that we all have had many experiences here on Earth and elsewhere. I am so glad that I had not been enchanted by the status of a "valued" profession, because I might be under that illusion today and my spiritual searching could have been stopped.

Many things that people interpret as outer and seen, really have to do with the inner and unseen. With the Age of Aquarius, the hippie generation took off their clothes, but the Age was about the unseen, not the seen. The Age was calling for a bare mind, an open mind, not a bare physical body.

When alchemists were trying to turn lead into gold, they mistakenly thought this was a physical formula, but it was a psychological one. They attempted to turn lead (soft and not pure), into silver (soft and pure), and finally into gold (hard and pure). A psychological movement was being revealed – from untruth to truth, from unconsciousness to consciousness. It had nothing to do with the physical metal, but what it symbolized.

Outer experiences are captivating, and people love the heightened emotions they gain from mountain climbing, deep sea diving, hang gliding, bungee jumping, ballooning and the like. Those of us who were old enough to remember were captivated with Apollo 11, when Neil Armstrong set his foot on the moon, July 16, 1969. However, it is the experience of inner space (the unseen) that brings the greatest high. The evolution of our species has to do with the exploration of the unseen, our inner space.

The unseen controls events. Have you wondered why things happen the way they do? Why does a person act that way? Why do some people get all the "luck?" *The Journey Home* by Lee Carroll, taken from knowledge of Kryon, states repeatedly, "Things are not as they may seem." The unseen is at work. What if everything that happens is part of a larger plan of which we are not aware in our limited consciousness? I am fond of the terms Divine Chaos and Divine Timing, both involving the unseen. Divine Chaos is especially interesting because it contains a duality. Our Higher Self/The All considers all things Divine, while our lesser self may call them Chaos. Levels of consciousness make the difference. Things appear chaotic because we don't see far enough.

I had an experience at the bank recently. The ATM wasn't working so I had to come back later. I was not pleased. When I came back to make my deposit, the woman before me had left her ATM card in the machine. I grabbed it and ran after her. It made me wonder. Was the reason I wasn't able to use the ATM before was so the timing would be right to help that woman? If this synchronicity didn't happen, how would it have changed her day? Her health? Her family?

What if all the experiences that cause us "difficulty" are for the good of ourselves or others -- avoiding a car accident, helping another, meeting or not meeting someone. The bank ATM is a simple example, but what I learned was when things don't go my way, it could be Divine Chaos at work, and a positive. If remembered, this concept could help me to stay positive in light of a potential negative. "Things are not as they may seem."

Kryon of Magnetic Service, states that 3D screams (the physical, the seen, the obvious, the linear), and spirit whispers (the emotional, the spiritual, the elusive, the unseen, the interdimensional). It is a profound change in consciousness when one wants to become aware of the whispers of the unseen. Some are born with that path. For others, it may take some kind of emotional jolt, such as a death or near death of one's self or a loved one, losing one's home in a fire, severe maiming in an accident, or any exaggerated situation that might cause them to re-evaluate life.

Dr. Jill Bolte Taylor, a Harvard trained brain scientist, tells of an extreme, shocking experience. She had a massive brain hemorrhage, and the left hemisphere of her brain, which handles the seen (the outer, the masculine principle), completely collapsed. During the hemorrhage, she was able to watch the process as her memory, motion, speech and self-awareness were shutting down. Suppressed by the blood clot, her mind went silent. Her consciousness shifted away from the reality her physical body was experiencing (the seen) and she entered the unseen, a "spiritual metamorphosis," a place of "inner peace and Nirvana," (the feminine principle).[5]

In a career that was dominated by the seen hemisphere, Dr. Taylor commented:[6]

> How many brain scientists have been able to study the brain from the inside out? I've gotten as much out of this experience of losing my left mind as I have in my entire academic career.

Because she completely lost the use of her left brain to handle anything seen, she only had use of her right hemisphere, and was able to discover the unseen. In *My Stroke of Insight*, she shares:[7]

> My right mind understands...that we are all connected to one another in an intricate fabric of the cosmos, and it enthusiastically marches to the beat of its own drum.
>
> Freed from all perception of boundaries, my right mind proclaims, "I am a part of it all. We are brothers and sisters on this planet. We are here to help make this world a more peaceful and kinder place." My right mind sees unity among all living entities, and I am hopeful that you are intimately aware of this character within yourself.

She acknowledges that people with normal brains can access their right hemisphere to find their own inner peace, improve their quality of life and the lives of others without having to go through such an extraordinary experience.

Do you ever feel that you are out of balance? Because of the nature of our society, most likely your left hemisphere is doing most the work. You may feel your activity has to match the fact that time is speeding up, and therefore, you must also. Activation of your right hemisphere by meditation and other relaxation techniques slows you down, and will help bring yourself back into balance. Your priorities may even change after giving the situation more thought.

We don't understand what we really are because we focus on the seen. We need to be in touch with the unseen, where the power is. Marianne Williamson in *A Return To Love: Reflections on the Principles of A Course in Miracles* states:[8]

> Our deepest fear is not that we are inadequate. Our deepest fear is that we are powerful beyond measure. It is our light, not our darkness that most frightens us. We ask ourselves, Who am I to be brilliant, gorgeous, talented, and fabulous? Actually, who are you not to be? You are a child of God. Your playing small does not serve the world. There is nothing enlightened about shrinking so that other people won't feel insecure around you. We were born to manifest the glory that is within us. And as we let our light shine we unconsciously give other people permission to do the same. As we are liberated from our own fear, our presence automatically liberates others.

Happiness is an issue of the unseen. We all know that the unseen is important or we would not be so interested in being happy. However, the road to finding happiness is misunderstood. Perhaps our forefathers did the country a disservice when they wrote in the Declaration of Independence that one of our rights was the "pursuit of happiness." Or, perhaps it was as it should be for us to wrestle with the issue of happiness so we can discover its true nature.

We search for happiness, but happiness can't be pursued directly, like a commodity. It doesn't matter what something is, you can be happy or not happy about it. Happiness is a decision, an attitude, a feeling. It should be en-lightening (lighten your spirit) to know that if you are unhappy, all you have to do is just change your attitude -- perhaps see the positive side, as the Yin Yang suggests. It's there.

An Old Tibetan saying acknowledges that happiness is not in the realm of the seen, but the unseen when it states, "Seeking happiness outside ourselves is like waiting for the sun to shine in a cave facing north." Again Lester Levenson in his book *Keys to the Ultimate Freedom*, 1993, reminds us: "If we don't like what's happening to us in the world, all we have to do is change our consciousness -- and the world out there changes for us."

I have been interested in meaning in my life, not happiness. I searched for meaning for a long time. I always thought it had something to do with what I was doing. It has been only in the last eight years that I realized that everything has meaning. I discovered that being is more important than doing, and being is what decides if something is meaningful. My Being decided that everything was meaningful, and it's the quality of mindfulness and presence with everything that gives meaning. I found meaning. Everything is filled with wonder and majesty. It is the sense that we admire in children with their awe and wonder.

I admire the shamanistic way of honoring all, thus acknowledging the respect and meaning for everyone and everything. Again, meaning is subjective, an attitude, and how one approaches something, not something objective. Everything has inherent meaning, and each person determines what it is for him or her.

Ignorance of the unseen keeps us from understanding others and our world. It's not what we see that controls us, but what we don't see. We have inner-eye blindness. We often "jump to conclusions" in situations and communications with our spouse, our children, and others. If we are aware, our inner eyes can pick up feelings from others and ourselves that reveal information much more important than words alone.

The following story is from Dharma teachings.[9]

> A teacher teaching Maths (sic) to seven-year-old Arnav asked him, "If I give you one apple and one apple and one apple, how many apples will you have?" Within a few seconds Arnav replied confidently, "Four!"
>
> The dismayed teacher was expecting an effortless correct answer (three). She was disappointed. "Maybe the child did not listen properly," she thought. She repeated, "Arnav, listen carefully. If I give you one apple and one apple and one apple, how many apples will you have?"
>
> Arnav had seen the disappointment on his teacher's face. He calculated again on his fingers. But within him he was also searching for the answer that will make the teacher happy. His search for the answer was not for the correct one, but the one that will make his teacher happy. This time hesitatingly he replied, "Four..."
>
> The disappointment stayed on the teacher's face. She remembered that Arnav liked strawberries. She thought maybe he doesn't like apples and that is making him lose focus. This time with an exaggerated excitement and twinkling in her eyes she asked, "If I give you one strawberry and one

strawberry and one strawberry, then how many you will have?"

Seeing the teacher happy, young Arnav calculated on his fingers again. There was no pressure on him, but a little on the teacher. She wanted her new approach to succeed. With a hesitating smile young Arnav enquired, "Three?"

The teacher now had a victorious smile. Her approach had succeeded. She wanted to congratulate herself. But one last thing remained. Once again she asked him, "Now if I give you one apple and one apple and one more apple how many will you have?"

Promptly Arnav answered, "Four!"

The teacher was aghast. "How Arnav, how?" she demanded in a little stern and irritated voice.

In a voice that was low and hesitating young Arnav replied, "Because I already have one apple in my bag."

During conversations, let's take some time to think about the apples that may be hidden.

In Robert Kiyosaki's, *Rich Dad, Poor Dad*, there is an example of a child who is asked what is 2 + 2. Is the answer always 4? Not necessarily. It depends if you are in base 10 or 2. When someone gives you an answer that is different from what you expect, try to suspend your judgment. There might be an angle that you have not considered. You must listen and understand with an open mind and an inner eye, for the unseen is at work.

Spiritualists and metaphysicians have said that until we start doing math in base 12 instead of base 10, we will not be able to understand the true nature of our DNA, and understand the full potential of the beings we really are.

As a stage actress, I learned that the unseen is in control. The audience comes to hear the subtext, not just the text. It is the feeling behind the words that gives the interest and the flavor to the script. There is a world of difference in a delivery that is full of color and one done in a monotone.

I have no idea where the saying came from, "What you don't know won't hurt you." It is so untrue. I experienced a glaring example of this right before I retired. I was head of staff at a University department and one of the employees in my supervision was stealing from the department. The amount of money was minor, but it hurt the department because we had to go through an audit. It also hurt me, because I didn't catch it right away. What you don't know *can* hurt you. It is wise to be aware of the seen and the unseen.

The legal system has it right; ignorance of the law is no excuse. The law still holds, and you are subject to it. That is why it is important to be aware of the unseen Universal Principles and Spiritual Truths. They are the rules of the game and they always apply. If you do not obey, you will pay a price. If it is an outer law, you may pay a fine or go to jail. If it's an inner law, "inner jail" results -- stress and dis-ease. Again, Dr. Wayne Dyer reminds us to "Row, row, row your boat gently, down the stream." Gently. Downstream. If you feel like you are swimming upstream, there is a principle or truth you are probably fighting. Look for the unseen.

In his book, *The Power of Infinite Love and Gratitude*, Dr. Darren Weissman states that all dis-ease comes from the inside out, from repressed negative feelings. The unseen is at work again with another case of "Resist not evil." The repressed emotion causes undo attention to it, resulting in stress. It is certainly accepted even in Western medicine that stress exacerbates any kind of unhealthy condition.

In an earlier chapter, I mentioned that I had breast cancer in 1996, and I knew I caused it. I was in a great deal of emotional pain to the point of considering suicide because of stress I felt because of my work environment. This stress caused my immune system to shut down and my body to go from an alkaline state to an acid one. Cancer cells only live in an acid environment. In a healthy immune system that is alkaline, the cancer cells cannot gain a foothold. Stress, because it causes the body to go acid, can cause cancer. It is crucial to discover and resolve the causes of any stress that you have; it can lead to life-threatening disease.

A documented study of the effects of emotion on the immune system was reported in the Journal of Advancement in Medicine (Summer 1995). The study, "The Physiological and Psychological Effects of Compassion and Anger," used the immune parameter S-IGA to test immunity levels. The study found that anger suppressed the immune system for five hours after the initial onset, and as the anger healed there was an increase of immunity for five to six hours.[10]

If one is aware of the unseen resistance (anger, hurt, non-acceptance) and is able to live with relatively little stress (healthy immune system), one can heal one's self. I had fibromyalgia for more than 25 years. Today, it is gone.
First of all, I am less stressed; I retired from the job. More importantly, I knew the power of the unseen and made decisions about where fibromyalgia fit in my life. It didn't. I knew that the disease served me in some way. I asked myself why I decided to get the disease and how it benefited me. I discovered I used the disease to get attention, sympathy and to avoid responsibility. I decided to give those up. I no longer

identify with the disease; it simply doesn't fit with my new being. I stopped the medication. I am free of it.

Candidly, I must add that I also used quantum knowledge, mentioned in the chapter on Oneness. Since time and space are one, I took myself back in time before the disease. To do this, one must have strong intent and belief that it is possible, and come from a base of love and not fear. Kryon calls this "Quantum Healing." It is using the more advanced dimensions of our DNA.[11]

Stress aggravates, if not causes many diseases, especially those of an autoimmune nature such as fibromyalgia, chronic fatigue syndrome, high blood pressure and various forms of arthritis and cancer. If you have one of these diseases, investigate the unseen. Think about why you decided to have it. How does it serve you? Do the disadvantages outweigh the advantages?

What are the causes of your stress? Stress means that you are "swimming upstream" against something. What are you resisting? What principles are you denying? Here again, the wolf has to be eaten. The three pigs did it. It is possible. The unseen principle, The Law of Attraction, popularized recently in The Secret, DVD, states that whatever you project out, you will receive in return. It is as reliable as action and reaction in the physical world.

Feelings and emotions have the power to control thoughts and actions. If you are angry, the outcome will be different than if you are accepting. The common saying is, "What goes around comes around." In the Bible (Galatians 6:7), Jesus said, "...Whatsoever a man soweth, that shall he also reap." If one sows corn, one gets corn, not wheat. If one sows positive, positive will be returned. If one sows negative, negative will be returned. It follows that it is best to never support a group that is ANTI anything. We are like magnets.

It draws the negative. Think again. Instead of being anti-war, be pro-peace.

The principle has also been called the Power of Positive Thinking, and many books have been written, including the well-known *Think and Grow Rich* by Napoleon Hill. This law is reliable as gravity.

Most of this is unseen and unconscious; we are not aware what we are drawing to ourselves. It is as simple as telling a child not to do something. What do they do? Exactly what you told them not to do. The psyche doesn't understand the words no, not, and don't. I catch myself when I am playing golf saying to myself, "I don't want to hit into the trees," and then I do. Or I think hitting to an uphill green is hard for me, and then it is. I am replacing these habitual thoughts with ones like, "I want the ball to go right there" and "I can do this." Now, I am aware of all the negative talk on the fairways; it is surprising to me that some people play as well as they do.

I also get a chuckle out of the "Easy Button" from Staples that says, "That was easy." I gave one to our son at Christmas last year, telling him it was one of the secrets to life.

Negative emotions (the unseen) are indicators that we are drawing negativity to ourselves and giving it power. The emotions of hate, fear, greed, jealousy, blame, and judgment are profound feelings that all of us are here to deal with in our lifetime. Mistakenly, we think by being angry or blaming that we are hurting the other person in some way. In reality, we are hurting ourselves and not them because they are in control of their own emotions. When we are aware that we are feeling negative (even more powerful than thinking), we can stop and replace it with a feeling we want. This awareness helps us flow with the positive principles in life. Then we are more in control of our lives, negating a stressful and victim scenario.

What we read and watch on TV is important. Filling our attention with people hurting other people takes a toll on us. We often become so used to it that we don't realize the harm it creates. Many women of my generation still remember the shower scene in the original Hitchcock film, Psycho. (And they re-filmed it!) When you experience something, it never leaves; it gets filed away somewhere in your brain.

The Law of Deliberate Creation is the term Abraham-Hicks (Esther Hicks channels non-physical being, Abraham) calls the method to help us get in control of the unseen. If we are not aware and deliberate about what we want to create, we are creating by default from old habits, memories and from the thoughts of others. Abraham-Hicks not only urges us to change in the moment as mentioned above, but also to set some time each day to be thankful for what we have and to project what we want. (If you don't know what you want, ask -- I want to discover what I want.) Do this about 15 minutes each day, then, move through your day believing and expecting to see what you desire. A finer point here is what Abraham-Hicks calls Segment Intending in which one identifies what one would like from each segment -- driving to somewhere (safely), talking with someone (harmoniously). My driving trips are much less stressful using Segment Intending.

There are some subtle caveats to this law that make it not as simple as it may seem. After the initial introduction of the Law of Attraction in The Secret, many gurus got on the bandwagon. But people found it was not that easy. What they were trying to attract was not happening, whether it was a dream car, a "soul mate," a new house, or a job.

One's subconscious plays a role here. You may want something consciously, but not subconsciously. You may be working against yourself, so your desire may not be forthcoming. What you think you want may not be the best for you in the long run, and a higher level may be at work.

Then, too, the universe favors the positive. If your reason for wanting something comes from love (help for the family), it is more likely to be realized than if it comes from fear (afraid for the family). Some have found the best way to approach a desire is to see in gratitude that it is already accomplished. Michelangelo spoke of creating the Madonna and Child in the Sistine Chapel. As he was working on it, he saw it as already accomplished, and he was merely uncovering it. (This concept was mentioned earlier in the section on the oneness of time and space.)

This chapter concerning the issue of the unseen has been just words; but to live beyond the physical seen is a quality of those who are in various stages of enlightenment. The unseen has traditionally been the realm and expertise of the Masters such as Jesus, Mohammed, Buddha, Lao Tzu, and of the Spiritualists. It is now spreading into the general population. An interest in the unseen has crept into our television viewing -- Haunting, Ghost Whisperer, Medium, Psych, The Mentalist, and Past Life.

In a humorous vein, a cartoon appeared in the Bay Area News Group, Contra Costa Times, Walnut Creek, California on 3/20/2008 highlighting the unseen.

MOTHER GROOSE&GRIMM (NEW) © GRIMMY, INC,
KING FEATURES SYNDICATE

Our consciousness and awareness of the unseen is rising. People are moving beyond the labels and roles of the seen. In his book, *The New Earth*, Eckhart Tolle examines the folly of living the life of the ego and outer identifications vs. the life of being. He urges us to look beyond our roles and titles to look at our essence. It is living in our essence that expands and enriches all that we do with our jobs and titles. Our essence is more mindful, more present, more aware, more creative, more conscious. Responding from essence, there is an increasing chance to discover the Oneness of All, and consequently, meaning, happiness and peace of mind.

How does one give attention to our essence? It is by quieting the mind, a challenging task. The mind wants to be in control. There is so much the mind wants us to concern ourselves with. Psalm 46:10 of the New International Version of the Bible states "Be still, and know that I am God."

Sathya Sai Baba reminds us:[12]

> The first step in spirituality is: Practising (sic) silence. Then, you can more easily recognize the galloping of the mind behind worldly happiness. Restrain its movements: turn it inside, into the calm lake of bliss that lies deep in the heart!

James Allen in *As a Man Thinketh* states:[13]

> Calmness of mind is one of the beautiful jewels of wisdom. It is the result of long and patient effort in self-control. Its presence is an indication of ripened experience, and of a more than ordinary knowledge of the laws and operations of thought.

Eckhart Tolle in *The New Earth* states that the profound is found between the spaces. It is our being that is found between our words.

The right kind of action needed on the planet comes from the unseen, an inner attitude of peace. Peace cannot be legislated or mandated. If we desire peace, we must look within and ask ourselves if we have a loving and peaceful nature. If the being is not right, the action won't be. One must rise above emotions and ideas that focus on the outer and those things that separate us. We must nurture the unseen. It is the new frontier that challenges us.

If for a moment we pretend that the little pigs had the DNA levels of a human being, what would they think about the seen and the unseen? They would know that the unseen was paramount. The unseen is what helped them survive that wily wolf. The clear thinking (the unseen) of the pig in that last house enabled him to set the kettle on to boil, knowing

that was the only way for the wolf to get into his house. Conquering the attitude of fear (the unseen) led to creative thinking (the unseen) and resulted in right action (the seen). All the other little pigs would have observed was the seen, the right action. The power that set the action in motion was all in the unseen. Comprehension of the unseen can lead to tasty rewards.

CAUSE AND EFFECT ALWAYS OCCUR TOGETHER

For every cause there is an effect, and for every effect there is a cause. Life is more understandable if one is aware that they can never be separated from one another. Many things become clear. "Chaos is only an illusion. It's what you see when you can't see far enough." (Deepak Chopra) Spirituality is practical because it enables one to see the cause and effect order in everything.

Causes produce effects. For instance, with our advancement in communication, news spreads worldwide immediately (cause). The effect is that newspaper companies and the postal service that still rely on the printed word are having financial difficulties, because their old methods are becoming obsolete.

Masaru Emoto, in *The Hidden Messages in Water*, gives an example of cause and effect, with the incidents occurring continents apart.[1] He writes that he was conducting water experiments in Tokyo when he recorded an increased value in the level of vibrations of elements that are harmful to the human body. He redid his experiments thinking that he had somehow made a mistake. It was not until the next day that he made a connection, when he read in the paper about the invasion of Iraq, the onset of the first Gulf War. The weight of the bombs that were dropped on that first day of the war was equal to all the bombs dropped in Vietnam. Those vibrations were carried by water almost immediately from Iraq to Japan and the rest of the world.

On a personal level, it can be difficult to see cause and effect. How many of us believe that we don't matter and our actions have no effect. We are just one individual and what impact do we make if we conserve energy or recycle our cans and bottles? The effect may be so small that we don't see it, but it still happens.

We make an effect whether we like it or not. Auras are measurable vibrations we emanate all the time, without even knowing it. We are surrounded by an even larger "divine light vehicle" (24 feet in diameter), called a merkaba, which cannot be measured by current instruments, but can be felt by others.[2] When we are aware that some people we avoid and others not, we are picking up the vibrations of their aura and merkaba.

Our past experiences and beliefs produce effects on our present lives. My husband and I participated in and led encounter-type groups with The Creative Initiative Foundation in the '60s and '70s. The focus of the foundation was to learn what it meant to love. Time was spent alone and in groups recognizing and resolving the negativity from our past that controlled us. We also examined whether loving attitudes were exhibited in the marriage. It became evident that if there were marital issues, they were more understood once a person's background and childhood were revealed.

Most issues have less to do with the actual situation at hand, and are more connected to a deeper root in the past, buried in the subconscious. Most psychologists tell us that we marry our partners to work out the relationships we have had with our father or mother.

Eckhart Tolle, in *The New Earth,* calls the hurtful experiences we have from the past, the "pain body." Others have said that someone "pushed their button."

Anger management courses, by definition, are designed to manage the effect (anger). Perhaps it might be more productive to discover what caused the anger in the first place. On a Dr. Phil show, there was an example of a man who became overly angry when he was watching football games on TV. After examining his background, Dr. Phil found that when the man was a teenager, he had accidentally run over and killed his pre-school sister. This "pain body" was activated while he watched sports on TV. It had little to do with the football game. Once this was discovered and the true pain handled, he no longer was angry during football games. This example shows why it is critical for psychologists to search for the true cause of the obvious effect with their clients, and not just try to change the effect alone.

Spiritualists say that it is possible that a behavior or feeling may not relate to one's current lifetime, but may have been seeded from a previous one. The term for this is "cell memory." The cells remember. (If time and space are one, that memory is still current.) Déjà vu is an example of this. I have a strong urge to jump when I am at high elevations. I wonder if I might have been one of those divers who dove into the ocean from a cliff?

Often people say, "I just don't understand why she (he) did that." The person is judging the other as deficient in some way. In reality, it is a lack of their own consciousness; they are really judging themselves for not understanding human nature, and the cause that produced the effect.

If there is always an cause that comes before an effect, does that mean there are no such things as "miracles?" Does this mean that nothing just happens by magic? Possibly. As St. Augustine said, "Miracles happen, not in opposition to Nature, but in opposition to what we know of Nature."

The universe is orderly because it is always in a cause and effect relationship. Miracles are instances where we haven't discovered the cause. Many inventions that we have today would have seemed like something from outer space at the turn of the century -- miracles. Explain faxes and computers to someone who was just experiencing the Model T Ford. I still am amazed at the telephone's ability to connect me with someone many miles away. And then, there is wireless. I remember a computer friend saying to me in the mid '60s that someday people will have computers in their homes. That seemed amazing, since at the time whole buildings were needed to house the workings of one computer. Today, many affluent households have a computer for each person, and laptop models for travel.

Might you consider a plane flying without a drop of fuel a miracle? One took off from Payerne, Switzerland, April 2010, on an around-the-world flight. Its name, Solar Impulse, gave the clue –- it was solar-powered.[3] However, currently it moves to slow for commercial use.

There is yet a higher level of awareness beyond basic cause and effect. The concept of cause and effect is valid, but it is linear thinking on a time line, that something came before and something came afterward.

What would it mean to think interdimensionally about this principle? It's more of a continuum and a circle than a before or after. There is no beginning and no end. (I'd heard that before, but I never really understood it until recently.) The beginning cause is the effect of the cause before it; the end

effect is the cause of what comes next. One would not be able to label any part as solely a cause or solely an effect.
Why does this matter? What might have seemed mysterious before, might be understood now. Look for the cause of the effect. It's there. Since cause and effect always occur together, here again is the concept that all is interconnected and all is one. Knowledge of Universal Principles and Spiritual Truths makes life more understandable.

What would the little pigs think about cause and effect? Because they don't have the DNA of humans, they live in that cause and effect world. They are not able to reflect on issues and understand them, just obey. We humans have the advantage that we can choose to live beyond animal consciousness. We are able to use our minds to investigate, evaluate, and understand truth. We are designed to operate and hold ourselves to a higher dimension than the physical, if we decide to do so.

TRUE FREEDOM IS AN INNER ATTITUDE

The wish for freedom has molded the history of the world -- freedom of speech, freedom to live where you choose, freedom of religious choice. Freedom is an issue that causes many world problems. People want to have free will; they don't want others controlling them.

Our Declaration of Independence sets out what our forefathers saw as the necessary freedoms -- life, liberty and the pursuit of happiness. People have expanded that list and want more things that symbolize freedom. Money is valued because it gives us choices and the freedom to buy things and travel. We focus on external things to gain physical freedom and end up fighting others to get them. Is there another aspect of freedom that is even more rewarding and longer lasting?

Spiritualists rhetorically ask, "What would true freedom be? What would it look like?" They respond: True freedom is an inner state of being that has nothing to do with external circumstances.

Formerly, I thought that one of the worst things in life would be to go to jail and lose one's freedom. But then I read Viktor Frankl's book, *Man's Search for Meaning*, and gained a different perspective. He was incarcerated in a Nazi concentration camp. In spite of this, he was able to find meaning there and not be in despair. They could not control his mind and his attitude. Could inner freedom be the truest freedom and more important than outer freedom?

Inner freedom allows one to be psychologically free, which means that no one can really do anything to you. No one can hurt the most important part of you, your spirit and soul, which is everlasting and not worldly. No one can hurt your feelings and make you angry. It is your own decision to feel that way. That's why some things make one person angry and do not affect another. You have a choice. It is empowering to know this and have it become part of your being. It is practical. You are in control of yourself and your own life -- that is true freedom. You are free.

Carlos Castaneda writes of Don Juan in *Journey to Ixtlan*,[1]

> The hardest thing in the world is to assume the mood of a warrior. It is of no use to be sad and complain and feel justified in doing so, believing that someone is always doing something to us. Nobody is doing anything to anybody. Much less to a warrior.

Inner freedom involves being free of the conditioning thoughts of the past, especially negative ones -- hate, guilt, fear, blame, regret, judgment, non-forgiveness. To be free of those is to live in a state of heaven on earth. Becoming free of negativity can be done through extensive therapy and soul-searching and/or can be done with the attitude that all is a positive learning experience.

It is our birthright to be in the state of inner freedom, which brings about thankfulness no matter what happens to us. Freedom is an inner knowing and an inner attitude and can be disconnected from the outer. Buddhist monks know this because no matter what happens to them, they say, "Thank you."

Freedom is being aware and choosing not to act from the basis of your ego self (what is best for only me), but from your true self, your everlasting self, your highest self, your part-of-God self, your being, your soul (what is best for others and the planet). Living in the higher self enables you to feel more open and less caught in a constricting, survival mode. More will be explored in the chapter "After the Principles."

True freedom also comes from aligning yourself with truth, what you can count on, and what always was, is now, and forever will be. In a visual way, it's like a tetherball attached to a pole that is the Principles and Truths. In junior high, I was hit severely by a slammed tetherball; after that I was always a little afraid of balls. I had always thought of that experience as totally negative. I would have never thought that the tetherball experience could have had a positive counterpart. Yet here it is, as an insight about true freedom (the Yin Yang affirmed again). The ball can swing with freedom and power because it is tethered and centered. The Universal Principles and Spiritual Truths steady and center your being.

Satya Sai Baba tells a story about free will in which people were flying kites. The kites soared to great heights, "darting and dancing in the heady atmosphere above the earth." Yet the kites seemed to struggle against their strings saying, "Let me go! Let me go! I want to be free." Finally one of the kites broke loose. "Free at last," it seemed to say. "Free to fly with the wind." We all know what happened to that kite. It "fluttered ungracefully to the ground, landed in a tangled mass, and was further tossed about by the strong wind." He reminds us that the restraints we often feel are the steadying forces that help us ascend and achieve.

Some reject the idea of restraints, rules, principles, all that is stable, because of the issue of "free will." Yet, there are some that are truly centering principles and truths, ones on which you can build your life, to build a house that will stand. They are the issues of the spirit, in the realm of the unseen. Part of my motivation in writing this book is to bring these principles and truths forward as an aid to those seeking true freedom.

Most of us don't realize that we may not be in jail, but we live in an "inner jail." We have food and exercise, but we are limited more than we know. We are still tossed around by what has happened to us in the past, what others think and say about us, from past values that we have not re-evaluated, and from being tied to our ego and wanting only what is best for us personally. But with awareness, we can break out of prison and have true freedom.

If one understood the pigs' story as symbolic, the focus of the book would lead to a different understanding. The meaning is internal, not external. Perhaps the pictures would have been given more attention than what the houses were made of; perhaps they wouldn't have been lost in later versions. The versions would also focus on the demise of the wolf and not find him running away. Because we focus on the outer vs. the inner, the story was not understood, was revised, and its powerful message was lost. Until now.

CHANGE IS A CONSTANT

Does the idea that things will change excite you? Are you apprehensive about change? The concept of change is often charged with emotion. If people have a fearful nature, they may feel threatened that things will get worse. If they have a hopeful nature, they may feel encouraged that things will get better.

What is the change about you might ask, because some changes can be more threatening than others. Does the change involve something that feels far removed, like an event in a foreign country, or does the change have to do with you personally and your close relationships?

I often remind myself that change is a constant, along with "Life is difficult," the first line of M. Scott Peck's, *The Road Less Traveled*. These concepts are so woven into our daily lives that we can't ignore them. Heraclitus (540 BC – 480 BC) said, "Nothing endures but change."[1]

Change is a constant -- a short but powerful statement. (This is different from the saying, "Change is the only constant." The Universal Principles and Spiritual Truths are constants, so change is not the only one.) Often we resist change, no matter what kind. "The beast we know is better than the beast we don't know."[2] How different life would be if we didn't resist change; we'd have less stress, for sure.

The world does not revolve around us, although we get set in our ways and expect stability. We need to be gentle with ourselves regarding change, to lessen the stress we feel. Change is about timing. We don't know enough and see enough yet. It is Divine Timing, and only the Divine (The All/our Higher Self/God) understands it.

Everything is changing; everything is evolving. There is a bias for increased adaptability and interrelationship. The Exploratorium in San Francisco, California has a demonstration called the "Living Beating Cells Floor Exhibit." It shows that heart cells beat independently, but, when two cells are placed next to each other, they coordinate to beat together and communicate with each other.[3] Interrelationship is in our best interest because all things are designed to work together, which is to be in the flow with the Universal Principles. Inwardly, it makes us feel good, safe, understood -- and loved.

The United States experienced so much change in 2008 and 2009 that most of us are still in some degree of shock. We had major changes in our elected officials, and massive changes in our economic and financial systems. Even though the changes have thrown our country into chaos, it could be called Divine Chaos. It's Divine because there is potential for great growth, creativity and vision. It's Divine because our planet is evolving from corruption and greed to integrity and responsibility. The change is positive, although it may not seem so now. Remember, chaos is what we call it when we can't see far enough.[4] When the chaos seems too much, too unsettling, we can remember the calming quote, "This too shall pass."[5]

During the election campaigns in 2007 and 2008, the word "change" was used so much it almost became a cliché. Everyone running for office was using the platform of "change." After the elections, it was still a catchword. At change.gov, one found the official website of Barack Obama's presidential transition project. (It was updated after the inauguration to whitehouse.gov.) It is a huge change to see our President sending out messages on YouTube and weekly addresses from whitehouse.gov. (Reminiscent of FDR's less frequent Fireside Chats?)

At change.org, you are asked, "What do you want to Change in the world?" This social network lets you "learn about causes, connect to good people and non-profits, and take action." You may have seen the commercials on TV around Christmas time, 2008, advertising the website, changingthepresent.org, where they showed women receiving special, loving gifts for others -- gifts of a polio vaccine, gifts of livestock. The ads have expanded to suggest this type of gift for other holidays and birthdays. This is a welcome change.

Do you think our political system needs to change? You may be interested in a new political party that has been formed. The Light Party with the ideal of "Health, Peace And Freedom For All," is a synthesis of the Democratic, Republican, Libertarian and Green parties.[6] They have formulated a 7-Point Platform to address and resolve our planetary challenges. It is so new that most people are unaware of it.

Another sign of change: An interest in looking for signs of life elsewhere in the universe is becoming more mainstream. In California, the SETI Institute and UC Berkeley's radio astronomy laboratory have set up a joint project.[7] "Telescopes in Hat Creek are designed to systematically scan the skies for radio signals sent by advanced civilizations from distant star systems and planets."

In Denver, Colorado, petitions were circulated for an initiative to be put on the ballot for an Extraterrestrial Affairs Commission.[8] "If approved, the city panel would promote 'harmonious, peaceful, mutually respectful and beneficial coexistence' between earthlings and extraterrestrials, in part by developing protocols for 'diplomatic contact.'"

Most of us are so caught up in our day-to-day lives that we don't think about alien beings or a time period longer than 100 years. We don't see the larger picture of change. Lately, however, there has been interest in the year 2012. December 21, 2012 is end of the Mayan calendar. Scientists tell us that on this date there will be a re-alignment of our planet, the sun, and the Milky Way that only occurs every 26,000 years. Many conjecture what this will mean for the planet.

The most profound changes we will be facing in the next few years will be these physical and psychological changes. The geological facts and possible consequences being reported might produce fear. The psychological and spiritual changes that are also occurring can enable one to live without fear, think clearly and maintain an inner peace no matter what occurs. It's similar to the last little pig awaiting the wolf. Some mystics believe the focused energy of the spiritual is the key and can alleviate the effects of the physical. What the physical and psychological changes may mean for all of us and the planet will be covered more fully in Chapter 13, The Future and 2012.

The three little pigs knew that change is a constant, or they would not have planned ahead to have that pot of boiling water ready. They prepared because they knew that, at any moment, change could happen. Otherwise, they might have just relaxed and rooted around as pigs do.

They ask if you are prepared for change, physically and psychologically. They urge you to be flexible and consider it an ally because -- change is a constant.

AFTER THE PRINCIPLES

Is knowledge alone ever enough? These principles are not new; they have been around for centuries. Without application, they are useless. Consider these intellectual principles; try them out; see if they ring true with your own experience. We know truths deep inside us, but often we need a hint or an experience to waken them.

I urge you to not believe anything just because it is written here (or actually anywhere). You have to experience the concept for yourself. Your own inner knowing is your best guide, not taking something on faith that is based on other people's experiences. Remember, their paths are not yours.

Abraham-Hicks states that words alone do not teach, that true knowing comes from life experience; a true teacher is one who stimulates your thinking.[12]

> ...'truth' is not found by going from teacher to teacher, church to church, or discipline to discipline, but by looking within the self. The intimate knowledge of consciousness, the 'secrets of the universe,' are not esoteric truths to be hidden from the people, then. Such information

is as natural to man as air, and as available to those who honestly seek it by looking to the source within.

After testing the truths, the challenging practice begins for those who are willing to take "the road less traveled." The practice can be quite a test of desire and stamina. To pull your self out of negativity, out of worry, out of fear, out of judgment, out of all that is not love can be an inner battle of major proportions.

Yet there is a reward if you are vigilant. It is possible to have a grateful and peaceful life, no matter what you experience. Sylvia Browne, teacher and psychic, says we are here to further perfect our soul. True inner peace may be what a perfected soul looks like. Dr. Peebles, as channeled by Summer Bacon in *This School Called Planet Earth*, sees the highest we can become as looking with "...loving allowance for all in their own time and place."[3] This attitude, which brings inner peace, relies on the ego-less mind and belief that "things will not always be as they seem."

Even those who consider themselves on a spiritual path and are attempting to align with the principles and truths, it is easy to be besieged by our own "humanness," our ego side, the part of us that wants to protect ourselves from hurt, anger and insecurity. There is a decision to be made. Who is to be in charge -- our ego selves or our higher selves? It is possible to decide and the effect is profound because the two sides are complete opposites. A change in who is boss can completely alter one's perspective and actions. The ego self is always in survival mode and wants to protect at all costs. This leads to fears, stress, insecurities, resisting change, blaming outer circumstances, avoiding difficult situations.

The higher self is the opposite, taking creative risk, understanding responsibility, having inner peace, feeling secure and not needing to protect and hide. Often, to transform from ego to the higher self, there needs to be a higher alignment in motivation from what is good for me to what is good for the whole and the planet.

With the latter, comes personal benefits, as a by product -- the benefit of being free to see clearly and to take appropriate action, the privilege of being happy, finding meaning, finding freedom and being a part of the wondrous evolution of the planet. We can join the creative minority of people who are bringing light to planet earth. This is a compelling undertaking for those who understand the implications of the Mayan Calendar and the year 2012.

And what about the little pigs? They applied their intellectual knowledge when they decided to eat the wolf. (I doubt that wolf was one of their common meals.) However, they were governed by their genetic code and didn't have an ego and free will like we do. Essentially, they never left the "Garden of Eden," where all was governed in perfect oneness. They unlocked the door to the principles and truths, but since they are not the primary actors on Earth, they can't unlock the evolutionary door.

Only you and I can.

2012 AND THE MAYAN CALENDAR

For the first time, we are seeing a coming together of science, religion and spirituality, acknowledging that energy is what we have in common, more than our physical world. These disciplines interconnect as they search together for the truth that binds us as one -- the answer to the conundrum of the Mayan calendar.

Spiritualists are interested in the calendar because of the potential they believe it predicts for the new world order of oneness for our planet. They look for the thinning of the membrane between the dimensions that will bring advanced spiritual information to those who are able to receive it. Hundreds of Internet websites in many languages and a growing number of books, videos, workshops and discussion groups speculate, sometimes wildly, about the Mayan calendar and the date, December 21, 2012, and what it will bring. Was the purpose of the Mayans to leave behind a definite set of clues and information about the nature and purpose of our planet and its time in the solar system and galactic field?

The Mayan civilization appeared "suddenly" in what is today

Mexico's Yucatan Peninsula, Guatemala, and parts of Honduras and Belize. They appeared to have arrived with an advanced technology already in place, rather than one that evolved over time.[1] Then, in the ninth century A.D., the Mayans suddenly abandoned their greatest cities. Experts may disagree on the mystery of their appearance and disappearance, but they can't argue about what they left behind -- the amazing and baffling Mayan calendar.

The Mayans did not follow our present Gregorian calendar because it didn't exist. They lived their lives based on three calendars. A solar calendar (365 days) and a ceremonial calendar (260 days), which together were called the Calendar round, and were a cycle of 52 years. They also had a "long-count" calendar based on five numbers that always individually totaled less than 20, which traced their mythical beginnings on August 13, 3114 B.C. and continued to December 21, 2012 (5,126 years).

This long-count calendar is the one that people refer to as the "Mayan calendar," that some say predicts the end of mankind. However, the Mayans believed that more dimensions of reality exist (the unseen) than purely the one of matter that we experience through our senses (the seen), so the calendar may be one of the birth and death of ages and not the physical. In numerology, the date December 21, 2012, adds up to 11/2, which is the Master Number of Illumination. This number denotes bringing spiritual truths to the universe and is the most insightful number of all in numerology. This may be an indication that around that date advanced knowledge may be passed from other dimensions to those who are able to receive it.

The interest in the Mayan calendar started gaining momentum at the time of the Harmonic Convergence, a term applied to the planetary alignment that occurred on August

16 and 17, 1987. Author Tony Shearer predicted the event in *Lord of the Dawn* in 1971. It was picked up and defined by Jose' Arguelles, Ph.D., academic and author, as[2]

> ...the point at which the counter-spin of history finally comes to a momentary halt, and the still imperceptible spin of post-history commences.

Believers in the prophesy of this new age of Convergence traveled to sites considered focus locations such as Mount Shasta, California; Stonehenge; Arizona; the Golden Gate Bridge; Bolinas, California; Haleakala, Hawaii; Crestone, Colorado; 2709 South Hawthorne in Kennewick, Washington; Dunn Meadow in Bloomington, Indiana; Paha Sapa, South Dakota; and Harney Peak (the Center of the Lakotan Universe), Custer State Park, South Dakota. Participants experienced collective prayer, song, meditation, dance, and ritual.[3] Many individuals taking part in the ceremonies claimed to have received divine guidance from the astral realms about the current state of Earth and the necessity of transformation. Many others made claims of personal transfiguration and revelation.[4]

Mystics have said that because of the number of people who were spiritual at the time of the Convergence, a shift happened for the outcome of the planet. The old prophesies of Armageddon were rescinded, and the planet would move from one of conflict into a global perspective of cooperation. It was the fulfillment of the prophecy of Quetzalcoatl, that following August 16, 1987, humanity would know and experience an unprecedented New Age of Peace, where many of the planet's "false structures of separation"[5] would collapse. Two years later, Kryon understood the time had come and started communicating with several spiritualists here on Earth.

Major change was experienced. In the 1980s and 90s, the world saw the breakup of the Soviet Union, the destruction of the wall that separated East and West Germany, and the end of apartheid in South Africa.

Some saw the movement as an announcement of the forthcoming end of time as we know it (linear time) and a preparation to move from third-dimensional reality of space into fourth-dimensional reality of time. Contrary to popular belief, it is time rather than gravity that keeps everything in the universe in order. Time is the mathematics of the universal laws of nature, the unifying force that holds everything together. The Mayans knew this, basing the Mayan calendar on the universal mathematics of the fourth dimension, (a 13:20 ratio vs. our 12:60 -- twelve months, 60 minutes per hour).[6]

Twenty-six years after the Harmonic Convergence, December 21, 2012, the Mayan calendar ends and a new 5,126-year cycle begins. Speculation is increasing as to what that rebirth holds. Are we headed for unprecedented catastrophe or 1,000 years of peace? Or both? There are three theories: 1. Catastrophic: a physical, global destruction, 2. Spiritual: a complete psychological transformation of mankind in which people will see themselves not as just "Homo sapiens," but "Homo spiritualist," and 3. Ongoing: a continuation of a spiritual process.

An unanticipated fourth possibility was reported December 21, 2009, timed well to be published exactly three years before the December 21, 2012 deadline.[7]

BIZARRO (NEW) © 2009 DAN PIRARO.
KING FEATURES SYNDICATE

There have been many end-of-the-world predictions in addition to the more well known, the book of Revelations and the predictions of Nostradamus. As early as 2800 BC, an Assyrian tablet was etched with words that they were in the "latter days."[9] More than 30 predictions have been documented predicting a timely demise of mankind, ranging from 365 AD up to the British sect, The Lord's Witnesses (March 21, 2008). They included dignitaries of various religions, astrologers, theologians, mathematicians, physicists, even Christopher Columbus and NASA scientist Edgar C. Whisenant (1988).[9] There have been more widely known groups that some have called Doomsday cults -- Jim Jones and the People's Temple in 1978, David Koresh and the Branch Davidians in 1993, and Heaven's Gate in 1997. And Hollywood had a creative time in 2009 depicting the destruction with its film, 2012.

Many hypothesize about the exact date of December 21, 2012. Jean Meeus reported in *Mathematical Astrology Marvels* in 1997 that the Mayans' calculation was off by 14 years. He attributes this to the fact that the Mayans didn't have telescopes and computers as we do today. That could have affected their calculation. If this is indeed true, the correct end of the Mayan calendar happened in 1998 and the shift would be over by 2012. Perhaps the shift has started and we are in the midst of it.

October 10, 2010 is an important date according to Starbird, a spiritual teacher and healer, channeling information from the High Council on Arcturus.[10] She was told starting on that date there will be great physical changes, with a polar shift in 2011, and the Earth will be quieting by January 3, 2012. All of this is to be happening before December 21, 2012.

On October 28, 2011, the planet will be ending the "Universal" wave, not December 21, 2012, according to Carl John Calleman, Ph.D.[11] He believes that, starting March 9, 2011, when the planet enters a "Galactic" wave, we will definitely start to feel a shrinking of the universe as the planet is preparing for the "Universal" wave that follows.

No one knows the exact timing or the nature of the physical changes that may occur, and whether or not they will happen in our lifetimes. What we do know is that changes are coming, and our beliefs and attitudes about them are crucial.

Peter Russell states that, since the emergence of Homo sapiens, we have gone through the Agricultural Age, the Industrial Age, the Information Age, and we are now in the time of the Wisdom Age.[12] He sees that in the Wisdom Age there are the "Half-Awake Species" and "Prophets of Wisdom," who are fully awake.[13] The latter are the enlightened ones -- the mystics, seers and saints who have in one way or another discovered and are at one with the true nature of consciousness and their being.[14]

In addition to predictions of significant physical changes on Earth by psychics and metaphysicians, there are scientific facts that cannot be ignored. A wide variety of scientists agree upon the following:

1. The end of the Mayan calendar marks a rare alignment of our planet, our solar system, and the center of our galaxy,

which will not happen for another 26,000 years. (Possible ramifications: change may have already begun.)

2. On March 10, 2006, a cycle of solar storms ended and a new cycle began. It is predicted to peak in 2012 with an intensity 30-50 percent greater than previous cycles. (Possible ramifications: The storms can affect all of our electronics, including our satellites and telecommunication systems.)

3. Scientists agree that Earth's magnetic fields are weakening quickly, and some suspect that we are in the early stages of a polar reversal. (Possible ramifications: Magnetism affects our nervous and immune systems; birds and ocean dwellers use magnetism for navigation.)

4. Correlations between the magnetic fields of the Earth and human experience suggest that it is easier for us to accept change and adapt to new ideas in weaker fields of magnetism. (Possible ramifications: This ability to change will help us as we encounter physical changes, and will help us with the need to work together for solutions. We have been in an "Information Age," with artificial technologies and artificial communication. Exactly what the "Age of Wisdom" holds is uncertain, but it will involve our own innate abilities, more than the use of devices. Some say they can feel the veil thinning already with information they are receiving from a higher dimension. The new ability may be the gift of our true selves.)

5. Recent validation of quantum principles proves that the way we perceive our world (our beliefs about our experiences) strongly influences our physical reality. (Possible consequences: How we experience change will affect the outcome. We will create the future.)

To date, the most current information comes from Kryon, channeled in the April 24, 2010 seminar in Mt. Shasta, California.[15]

He tells us that the weather changes we are seeing now are not a surprise; it was prophesized (by him) 21 years ago. He saw that the "consciousness shift taking place on this planet was so great that it would effect the dirt of the earth." What we are seeing are the changes in the water cycle (ice/water). It has happened over and over, and is not new or exceptional. The last one was in the 1400s, and "they are so slow there is no remembrance...of them and the time span is so great that the record keeping does not exist in the form it is today." In the 1400s, there was a mini ice age and we are going through that again. "There is no need to fear; all you have to do is recognize it and get out of the way." With the ice melting, there is a shift in weight so there needs to be a readjustment in the earth's crust, and that is what is causing the earthquakes and volcanic eruptions. The warmer water is also intensifying the storms.

He further states that we have lost our appreciation of Mother Earth (Gaia). If we are able to raise our vibration and relationship of appreciation for Mother Earth, we will be able to influence the weather. He asks each of us if we have a relationship with Gaia. Can we give instructions for Gaia to shake less in areas that are populated? "Conscious over matter. It is a relationship with a planet that wants to hear from you. ...Re-establish the relationship and watch what happens."

Eckhart Tolle sees the shift's emergence.[16]

> What is arising now is not a new belief system, a new religion, spiritual ideology, or mythology. We are coming to the end not only of mythologies but also of ideologies and belief systems.

The change goes deeper than the content of your mind, deeper than your thoughts. In fact, at the heart of the new consciousness lies the transcendence of thought, a newfound ability of rising above thought, of realizing a dimension within yourself that is infinitely more vast than thought.

Some have said during the time of the shift that everything would be chaotic until natural forces would restore the balance of life. To date, there certainly is chaos everywhere -- the world financial system, deficits in U.S. cities, the housing market, the high U.S. unemployment rate, and unstable foreign governments, currencies and our weather.

It is a time of planetary change, not just national change. Some people were upset when, on the campaign trail, Senator Barack Obama referred to himself as a "world citizen" versus a U.S. citizen. Gregg Braden agrees that we must move beyond our limited thinking.[17]

> Nationalism is becoming extinct. It happened to the dinosaurs. And it happened to the Neanderthals. The wheels of the power train are going to leave the tracks. This is a process, however, and not to be taken personally. Also, be careful not to assume an attitude that some of us are better than others. It only means that the people in power are going to get more and more frantic as these changes occur and will either have to change their ways or be run over. It is a fact that ethical consciousness must be in place before we can go into the consciousness of co-creation. Right now, do you trust your neighbor to be able to create anything he wants in your back yard? Obviously we are not there yet

> We are living in a world of the "mass mind," which is controlled and manipulated by governments and institutions. Mass media continually dispenses information of a negative nature. We are in the grips of "cultural hypnosis or a civilizational trance."[18]
>
> We must go beyond technology. ...In terms of Spaceship Earth, the wrong crew is in command, and it's time for a mutiny.

There are signs of mutiny. The movie, The Shift, is a case in point. Craig Hamilton, one of the story editors for the movie, held a free teleseminar recently, "The Key to Evolving Beyond Ego: How to Make the Change that Changes Everything." Four thousand, three hundred people signed up, and more than 35,000 people downloaded the recording in the four days afterwards. (The "Change" involved your motivation for your own personal growth. Was the focus for your benefit alone, or to enable you to be a service to others?)

The growing positive is a beautiful thing to watch unfold. As What the BLEEP....? reminds us, we have to believe in it and look for it to see it. Most of it is in the realm of the whispers of the unseen.

The three little pigs would support the mutiny. They wouldn't want any variety of wolf (physical, mental, or emotional) threatening their homes, their oneness, their inner peace, their being. It is a mutiny not like any other. The movement is toward something positive for the planet and is not against anything (resist not evil). Some in the movement call themselves "evolutionaries."

How do you feel about evolutionaries and the mutiny?

CALLING ALL EVOLUTIONARIES

The call went out at the time of the Harmonic Convergence, and people are responding in many ways.

I receive unsolicited religious pamphlets and newspapers several times a month. Because they are usually highly judgmental and dogmatic, I throw them away immediately. Something made me look at *America's Good News*. Perhaps it was the capitalization and size of the typeface on the lead article, "RELIGIOSITY, IS IT KILLING THE CHURCH? PRISONERS FROM WITHIN." And within the article, in red, it states:[1]

> The religious spirit, in its fullness, is like the sheep in wolves clothing. From the outside it seems to love God but festering on the inside is such hideous things like pride, judgment, comparison, and bitterness.

Is this a creative minority seeing that one's inner being and how one treats one's fellow man might be more important than outer memberships and affiliations? If so, the paper is aptly named; it *is* America's good news.

Throughout history, benevolent creative minorities have accomplished the most positive changes, the fully awake leading the half-awake. More people are discovering and practicing the concepts of the Universal Principles and Spiritual Truths in their daily lives, for their own well-being and for the love of the planet. They may call it ascension, beingness, at one with God, I am that I am, enlightenment, walking the road less traveled, going through the "eye of the needle," At-one-ment, a Lightworker, a Mystical Traveler, or an Evolutionary.

This increasing minority will gradually generate enough power to shift the balance on the planet from duality to oneness. Kryon of Magnetic Service's figure is one half of one percent of the population, which would be approximately 34 million people.[2]

On the Internet at worldwidetippingpoint.com is a "visual reference, a 'Counter,' for the rapidly growing movement for the 'transcending change' happening all over the Planet." The goal is to "motivate 100 million people to sign The Counter, with the intention that this number represents a critical mass of people sufficient to tip the scales to a greater future. They also offer "special tools, services and products that can help YOU be the change that is happening, and inspire you to become an active participant in the great shifts occurring throughout humanity." Included is a report, "7 Powerful Techniques To Help You Shift (in a Rapidly Shifting World)." They quote Thomas Paine, who wrote during the American Revolution, " 'we have it in our power to begin the world over again', and that is exactly what people living on this planet right here, right now have the opportunity to do!"

Among some of the Internet groups helping people to communicate with each other are Grace Light Global, Inner Talk, Integral Enlightenment, EnlightenNext, Integral Life,

New Earth Center of Light, Healing Humanity and Healing International.

Heavenly Light Emporium, states:[3]

> "We are All One. I love You!" is the Supreme Mantra for these times and the daily practice of this Truth is the key to ascension (living in inner peace and love) in this lifetime! We are literally reprogramming the consciousness of humanity from fear into Love while helping to heal Gaia, our benevolent hostess (Mother Earth) and all Life on Earth.

ONEVOICE, a grass-roots movement to end the Israeli-Palestinian conflict, began in 2002.[4] They claim that the real struggle is not between the Israelis and the Palestinians, but between the moderates and the extremists. As of April 2010, 74 percent of Palestinians and 78 percent of Israelis are willing to accept a two state solution. At their website, www.onevoicemovement.org, you can endorse their effort in various ways, including being an "international supporter."

Humanity's Team Worldwide is collecting at least 50,000 signatures as part of a campaign to appeal to the United Nations to declare a Global Oneness Day. Hopefully, by the date this book is published, they will have reached their goal.[5]

It was the tales of near-death experiences that originally wakened me to the fact that there is much more going on with life than appears on the surface. With the shift in the age, more people are receiving information from non-physical beings who encourage this positive mutiny. These experiences are difficult to dismiss. In a personal experience, I was given knowledge of an event before it happened, saving me from a serious automobile accident. Also, my book's manuscript was protected by an "alert" to watch out for a possible spill on my laptop computer. I was prepared, and there was no damage when it happened three minutes later. These were much more than just intuition; I saw a brief glimpse of it happening.

And there is the little boy who said he was whisked away by the "birdies" from the garage door that was closing down on him. A friend of mine told me of his own rescue by "something," that picked him up from the middle of a lake where he was drowning and put him on the opposite shore.

There are people who have been called to help the planet bring in the new world order. These people act as lighthouses, to shine light so that others may see. Not everyone needs to be a lighthouse. The important thing is that there is enough illumination so that others may find the way.

Here is the story of Shelley Yates, who organized FIRETHEGRID. She reported that she died with her son in a flooded car and was visited by a Being who brought her back to life. This Being also gave her new information as to how to heal her son and the world. She relates in LIGHT & LOVE, A GIFT FROM THE STARS: [5]

> My name is Shelley Yates and my star name is Samoiya. I was granted the gift of intuitive sight after a death experience in which my four year old son and I were drowned in a flooded car.
>
> I was an angry, hostile, unhappy person the day my car hydroplaned into that flooded marsh and the cold black water took my life and the life of my sweet baby boy. I was granted a visit from a magnificent Light Being who would change my

life. I was submerged in that murky water for over 15 minutes and my son was without oxygen for over 30 minutes. This magnificent Light Being stayed with me as I died then told me of the future and how I would be given information to save my son's life.

When I arrived at the hospital, I found my sweet boy connected to every machine imaginable. The doctors told me to have no hope for in their opinion my son was already dead and there was nothing I could do except unplug him and let him pass peacefully. The Being from the car came to me again and told me how I could transfer body energy from other loving humans and infuse that same energy into my little boy's body. It was just like a blood transfusion only better! I followed the instructions given to me and in three days my son came back to me, whole and healthy. I have been blessed to have my son returned so I can share many more precious years with him.

Perhaps this story touches me because of our experience with our dying son, when my husband and I beamed light to him. Perhaps it was our transference of body energy, and that of other adults and children that helped him live.

She continues:[6]

> I have also been given additional information to aid in the healing of the earth, wonderful news to unite humanity as one race with peace and prosperity for all. I was told by the same Light Being "What you did for a dying boy with a small group of people you can do for a dying planet with a much larger group."

> I was directed to perform a massive energy transfusion for the earth and her inhabitants by assembling a mass edition globally with hundreds of thousands of loving humans each contributing their energy to heal the earth and catapult it into the new time of Aquarius. This is the dawn of a new era where we, as a dedicated group of humans will forge a sharing mentality that will change the earth's course and its outcome. We are all entities of Divine Grace and are therefore entitled to co-create through intention that which will bring us our greatest joy. This project can be found online at www.FIRETHEGRID.org....

In the '70s, while working with The Creative Initiative Foundation, we talked about the cloistered nuns whose sole purpose it was to pray for the planet. Fire the Grid gathered millions of people from over 92 countries on July 17, 2007, and July 28, 2009. Together, they transferred energy to heal the Earth. The final time for the gathering will be November 11, 2011, 11:11 GMT. These were the specific dates given by Shelley's guides.

She continues:[7]

> ...As the earth travels within our galaxy, we as a group of humans living on this earth are moving into a photon belt in the Milky Way. This is a matter of physics and physical fact. The poles of this earth are shifting and there is much unrest on our planet today.
>
> ...These wondrous Light Beings have educated me to the fact that the human flesh we live in is programmable. We are ultimately responsible for the day-to-day programming of this body that we

live in, and it is with each thought and belief that we do just that.

...It has been explained to me that a shift is happening within our earth field and that we must attune to a new level or we will find it difficult to assimilate this higher, less dense frequency. There is no judgment attached to this happening, however if we are to live here in comfort, we will need to lift the frequency within our own field to match the (higher) frequency of the energy here on the earth plane.

The energy field that lives around each human holds a vibrational signature that indicates where we live in this time and space. It is like a fingerprint as it is our mark on the earth grid that surrounds our planet. Where you live in the vibrational field dictates whether or not the human body can adjust to what is coming. Many New Age Metaphysicists are calling this new time and frequence the "Awakening" or the "Ascension" process. It is a spiritual event that has been prophesized for eons. I am telling you that no matter what you call it; it is coming. These beings simply want to assist with this time transfer.

She adds:

...The winds of change can be directed and this is our opportunity to consciously choose that direction.... We must align in our similarities and not dissolve in our differences.... There are enough of us to charge every positive thought possible. Each one of these thoughts will then be inserted into the energy of the planet. There are more humans awake and aware than ever before in the history of our time here on earth.... As each of us as individuals see the earth in its true potential, collectively we will begin to create a world with untold possibilities.

Thank you Shelley for your life path as a messenger.

A similar message to gather people together was given to Jonathan Goldman, Healing Sounds pioneer and international acclaimed author. He believes: [8]

There is a prophecy leading to 2012 that suggests when people sound together with their voice as a singing prayer for world peace and harmony, it can have a significant effect in restoring peace on earth. ...With our wisdom and intentional sound, we can affect dire 2012 predictions in a helpful way -- The Way of Compassion, Love and Lasting Peace.

His group, Healing Sounds, organized The World Sound Healing Day 2010, on February 14. It was five minutes of toning and chanting at noon, Eastern Standard Time, where thousands throughout the planet joined for the eight annual Sonic Meditation for Peace on Earth.

Dr. Carl J. Calleman organized a "Consciousness Convergence," for July 17-18, 2010, a type of follow-up to the Harmonic Convergence. He says people were urged to "create an intention for the planet to manifest a unity consciousness beyond that of duality."[9]

Neale Donald Walsch sums up the focus, values and nature of those on the "road less traveled." He states that these people base their lives on principles and truths that are timeless and forever true. Because of this, their thoughts and actions enable them to be a Light to the world.[10]

How to be a Light...

> Embrace every circumstance, own every fault, share every job, contemplate every mystery, walk in every man's shoes, forgive every offense (including your own), heal every heart, honor every person's truth, adore every person's God, protect every person's rights, preserve every person's dignity, promote every person's interest, provide every person's needs, presume every person's holiness, present every person's greatest gifts, produce every person's blessing, and pronounce every person's future secure in the assured love of God.

There are lightworkers and evolutionaries on this planet right now. Most are "normal" people with advanced understanding and being. They are both male and female, different ethnicities, different religions, different economic circumstances, in different countries. What is more important about them is not the outer identifications, but their inner qualities of understanding and compassion -- of love.

They are on a "Lightworker Path," not claiming that they have arrived at any heightened point. They aim for a state of consciousness that is almost devoid of negativity, because they see, as Yehuda of the Weekly Kabbalah Tune Up (Internet site) states: "The pleasure we get from judging, hating, raging, abusing, neglecting, demeaning, hiding, is a tiny drop of death energy."

They know that all people, no matter who they are or what they do, deserve love, because all are eternal souls and part of God. They aim to honor all people and animals in their own place and time and treat all that is in the physical world with care and non-judgment. They know that all is in a state of perfection and often they don't see the whole picture so their judgment might be flawed. Lightworkers are more concerned about how they can serve others, than for their own ego wants and needs. (They understand the third house of the little pigs and the right relationship with people.) They live in forgiveness, knowing that forgiving has little to do with an event or another person, but is an issue with themselves.

They live in gratitude, being able to transform the "negative," by seeing it as merely half of the whole, a learning, a blessing. They do not see something as a "waste of time," knowing all is important and perhaps the lesson to be learned has not yet shown itself. For them, meaning is everywhere and each person and event is a chance for greater learning and understanding. They understand the flow of BE DO HAVE and understand that the physical and doing (per se) are not the goal. They acknowledge that everything comes from the inner, the being, and if the being is not of love, no matter what one does, the outcome will hurt someone.

One doesn't have to be a Jesus or a Buddha or a Gandhi. They had it perfected, were "fully awake" and are guides. Most of us are "half awake" and in process if we decided to take the "road less traveled," the road of "resist not," the road of acceptance, the higher road, the road of the love of God. In simple terms, they know and practice the Universal Principles and Spiritual Truths. Those on this path see a new species of human being born (a rebirth) that psychically forms a new community of people, who are changing the focus and future of this planet.

The Intenders of the Highest Good proposed a new holiday -- Global Observance Day. It is not one specific date, but a date that each one of us would choose. They suggest: [11]

> Pick a day -- any day you like -- and for as long as you can remember to do so, simply observe what goes on around you (hence the name Global Observance Day).
>
> On this day you're not going to judge, label, categorize, analyze, record, or even give a name to anything in your immediate world. Likewise, you needn't believe, accept, reject, or react to anyone else's ideas unless you want to. All you have to do is witness what's going on.... After you get good at impartially observing your outer, worldly surroundings, then go on to observing your inner thoughts without judging them.
>
> If you notice at anytime throughout the day that you've slipped back into judging or labeling things, be easy on yourself. Don't browbeat yourself—simply start over with your impartial observing. Even if you have to begin anew a hundred times over the course of the day, that's okay.
>
> Eventually your perceptions will shift and when you least expect it, you will step into a world that was unavailable to you when you were putting your spin on everything.
>
> You'll get a glimpse of the world as it really is, where everything is connected to everything else, where everything glows, and where you know you are part and parcel of a Great Oneness that has been there all along.

From that point on, you'll be less apt to harm or judge anyone every again because you'll know that you would only be harming of judging another part of yourself.

No wrong, no right
No dark, no light
No good, no bad
No sad, no mad

No low, no high
No yours, no my
No rich, no poor
No less, no more

No weak, no strong
No short, no long
No big, no small
No spin at all

No there, no here
No far, no near
No gain, no name
It's all the same
It just is.

If the three little pigs were able to look beyond their walls today, they would see that we are in the midst of a shift. They would see increasing consciousness and good will on the planet. If you look beyond your walls, you will see it too. The light beckons to you and welcomes you.

EPILOGUE

THE CHALLENGE TO LOVE IS BEFORE US

The Three Little Pigs is just a fairy tale. What we face in these next years is real. There might be changes at a rate that we have never seen before. This fairy tale and the Universal Principles can give us insights that could be needed for our very survival, psychologically and physically.

Our decision to come to this planet was profound. We did not have to do this. We all decided we wanted the chance to see if we could turn all of the experiences we have here into those of love. This is the further perfection of our soul that we desired.

However, can we look beyond the allure of the physical world and remember who we really are and why we came to Earth? It can seem like a daunting task, more than any outward accomplishment. It takes psychological courage to be different and to take the inner road rather than the outer. Few of us are willing to see the value and to take the journey.

We are fortunate that we chose to live during powerful times, when time itself is challenging us to live at a higher dimension. Evolution has brought us helpers that believe and love the journey of the unseen. The change from duality to oneness is happening now, as lightworkers and evolutionaries with help from non-physical beings raise the consciousness of the planet to meet the challenge.

> Nothing is more powerful than an idea whose time has come.[12]

It is exciting.

It is powerful.

It is our destiny.

It is now.

Blessings to you on your path,
Patricia Pillard McCulley

APPENDIX A: *LIST OF UNIVERSAL PRINCIPLES*

#	Principle	Intellectual Knowledge	Experienced Emotionally	Origin
1	We are spiritual beings having a human experience, not human beings having a spiritual experience.	Y	Y	Gnosticism
2	Everything exists in perceived opposites. (Yin Yang)	Y	Y	Tao
3	Everything is connected. We are all one.	Y	Y	Science/Spirituality
4	There is always cause with effect and effect with cause. (no miracles?)	Y	Y	Creative Initiative/ Tao
6	The unseen is more important than the seen.	Y	Y	Spirituality
7	Change is a constant.	Y	Y	Fact
8	Movement is from simplicity to complexity to simplicity.	Y	Y	Creative Initiative
9	Matter is never destroyed, just changes form.	Y	Y	Science

10	Everyone's purpose in life is the same and different.	Y	Y	Gnosticism
11	You can reliably count on and base your life on the Universal Principles. (vs. money, physical, family, people, status etc.)	Y	Y	Insight
12	When you are grounded (your life is based on universal principles), you are free.	Y	Y	Insight
13	There are forces outside ourselves, which are more powerful.	Y	Y	Religions/Spirituality
14	After death, there is an Other Side, where all will be understood, joyful, and peaceful.	Y	N	Gnosticism
15	Our lives--happenings, numerology numbers, events--have been planned by us on the Other Side before we came to Earth to teach us lessons, to perfect our souls, to remember who we really are.	Y	Y	Gnosticism / "Conversations with God" By Walsch/ Intuition
16	We have lived many lives on Earth and other places.	Y	Y	Gnosticism
17	If you do not go within, you are with out.	Y	Y	Gnosticism

18	Be-Do-Have is the correct flow and not the reverse.	Y	Y	"Conversations with God"
19	We do not need anything (need is an illusion).	Y	Y	"Communion with God" by Walsch
20	Resist not evil. Stop the stopping. (Respond)	Y	Y	Jesus, Zen B, Walsch
21	Each person is solitary.	Y	Y	Gnosticism
22	Psychological pain is the result of not accepting a truth/reality.	Y	Y	Creative Initiative
23	True faith is understanding a principle intellectually, but not seeing how it applies in a certain case or any case.	Y	Y	Creative Initiative
24	Highest emotion is compassion.	Y	Y	Buddhism
25	Where there is anger, there is hurt and vise-versa.	Y	Y	Creative Initiative
26	Every experience we have is meant to lead us to a greater sense of spirituality in our lives.	Y	Y	Various
27	There are no accidents or coincidences.	Y	Y	Gnosticism
28	A peaceful world is gained by people having an absence of inner fear and greed.	Y	Y	Insight

29	God is dual; Two entities--Man and Woman.	Y	Y	Gnosticism
30	The inner controls the outer.	Y	Y	THE SECRET, Gnostics
31	We are in charge of our own feelings and emotions. No one makes us feel anything.	Y	Y	Psychology
32	Row, row, row your boat, gently down the stream	Y	Y	Dr. Wayne Dyer and Nursery Rhymes
33	Good and evil are subjective.	Y	Y	Various

NOTES:
1. This list, developed from the 1960s to 2007, was the basis for this book.

2. Creative Initiative was a religious educational group I worked with during the '60s and '70s. We studied world religions, the actual teachings of Jesus, and put ourselves through intensive psychological work to start a process of ridding ourselves of all negative emotions toward people and happenings in our lifetime.

3. The principles are in no special order.

4. Walsch=Neale Donald Walsch

5. The Secret is a DVD.

6. What started me on a quest for these was a book of Moody's I read in the '60s where a person came back after having a near death experience, and he was asked:
   1. Did he learn how to love and
   2. Did he know the Universal Principles?
I decided that it would be important in my life to search for the Universal Principles.

APPENDIX B: *LETTER TO MY SON, 1986*

February 11, 1986

Dear Matthew:

In response to your offer, here is what I would like you to pass on to your children from me. The concepts embodied in the Yin-Yang.

1. Everything in life is made up of dualities, opposites: high-low, hot-cold, birth-death, good-evil, fear-courage, masculine-feminine, despair-hope, cause-effect, conscious-unconscious.

2. Within each is the intimation of the other.

The Yin-Yang contains universal principles that work all the time. They are in effect all the time even though we are not aware of them. To be aware and to put trust in them (even though you might not see how they apply at first) bases you in what is real and what you can depend on. Principles like these are the only things you can really count on and depend on in life; they are the basis of true security (not $$, not looks, not your mind, not possessions, not friends, etc.) and cannot be taken away from you.

The principles within the Yin Yang are not really practical unless you understand how they apply to everyday life, that is -- what does this have to do with me and living. (This information is to be passed on also -- including examples of your own.)

What are the ramifications?

1. Nothing that happens is solely good or bad. It contains both, maybe more of one than the other, but both are there.

It is only that our perception is limited, when we only see one part. Common expression -- "Every cloud has its silver lining." Helps you to accept the negative more easily and not get so depressed.

    a. Whenever something bad happens, knowledge that it's not all bad helps a little and can enable one to refocus and look for the positive. "When one door closes, another one opens."

    b. When something good happens, knowledge that it's good but "everything has its drawbacks" helps when the negative in it surfaces and it will eventually. Helps you from becoming depressed and regretting the circumstances when the positive bubble bursts.

2. As applied to people, no one is just good or bad, but we all have both, albeit hidden. Most people do not show/are not aware of their full selves. What you are not aware of controls you, not you it. As you are aware of both sides, you are able to more easily understand and accept yourself and others. Enables you to become an understanding, compassionate person and one who can be perceptive with people and remain objective and not get caught up oneself in the other person's problem. Incidentally, to be aware of your full self doesn't mean you have to act on it (i.e., your negative).

    a. This knowledge helps when one is (theatre) acting. Within a person is everything, every person, every act, every feeling, every possibility. "There but by the grace of God, go I." To do a role, one just has to tap in to that part of oneself.

    b. What we show to others is our decision. And often what is shown on a person's facade is the opposite of what they are down deep (and is controlling them). A too sweet person has negative thoughts too -- what does he/she do with them? "Killing with kindness"? A hard, mean person often is covering up a dear, "too tender" soul. The most trustworthy person is one who shows both sides (in moderation), for that person is more likely to be in control of both and not go overboard either way.

My personal examples of these concepts are not necessarily to be passed on: (better to pass on your own)

1. My first real awareness of how these concepts work came while reading the book *The Hiding Place* by Corrie Ten Boom about Nazi concentration camps. This one woman was interned in a barracks that was terribly infested with fleas, and the women were badly bitten. (This situation with fleas seems especially negative to me since I hate fleas and bites so much.) While there, the women were trying to discuss religion and the Bible, which was not allowed. Despite the flea irritation, Ms. Ten Boom accepted the flea situation. She had the faith that fleas were not all negative; there was a positive side, even though she was not sure what it was. Later she found out the reason they were able to have those secret religious discussions was that the guards stayed away because the fleas were so bad in that particular barracks. Point: positive of the fleas and confirmation of the wholeness.

2. This example is more personal for me and cemented the Yin-Yang principles into my psyche and soul forever. I struggled with the Yin-Yang when you were hurt, Matthew. Positive in that? Forget it -- yet I knew the principles to be true; I put my faith in them. ("Don't put your faith in a chair that's not there." Harry Rathbun, a leader in Creative Initiative) I think the most secure meaning of faith is not when you don't know if it's true and you just hope it is, but to know a principle works, but maybe in this exact situation you don't know how it works specifically.) And I knew I could not be really supportive to you and I knew my own personal pain

would not end unless I saw the whole picture. So I kept thinking and praying about that small white dot on the black side, which I hoped would lead me to the large white half. It took me two weeks to find the white (positive) and to make the experience whole for myself. Are you interested in what I saw the positive to be? It was a combination of a couple of things -- that quality is more important than quantity. You had given so much in your short life as evidenced the way your friends expressed their good feelings about you. I hoped that I could give that much in my in my whole lifetime as you did in your short one. After all, isn't that what life is all about?

And, you taught so many people the "right" way to pray. The highest form of prayer is not to ask for what you want to happen. (After all, it would not be all positive. Besides how are you to know what is best in the long run.) The highest form is to state your preference knowing you are not in charge and acknowledging that you are willing to accept whatever will happen, and to see the whole picture.
Other positive aspects were that I also learned to never take anything for granted again -- makes me more appreciative of life and normal, everyday things. I gained an extreme appreciation of how fragile and complicated the human body is. "There is no free lunch." No medicine or treatment is altogether positive, there are always drawbacks. And as for the negative aspects of the whole accident, that was fairly obvious.

More esoterically, the concept of the Yin-Yang answers for me, the question that is asked so man times "If God is good, why does He allow evil in the world?"

1. There is no such thing as absolute evil. To disallow something that is evil, one is also disallowing the good part of it.

2. What is evil to one person, another may perceive as good. Because of everything's dual nature, we can choose to see of emphasize only part of it and call it "good" or "evil."

3. God does not manipulate things. Laws of nature are already set and dependable (cause and effect); we may just not see the whole picture. Man is the only actor on the earth and he too is totally predictable given his background (if only we could really understand it).

Matthew, there are few things as important as this for me to give you and your children. The hope for the planet is that we learn from each other and each generation progresses positively beyond the other. Thank you for this opportunity.

Love,
Mom

APPENDIX C: *LETTER TO MY SON, 2009*

May 16, 2009

Dear Matthew:

This is intended to be a follow up to the letter I wrote you in 1986 about what was most important to me, which was about the concept of duality.

You commented to me recently that I seemed to be able to control my emotions when talking about a subject, and that you had more trouble with that. In the book I am writing, there is a sub-chapter about this issue, called "Beyond the Opposites."

It is our destiny here on earth to move beyond the opposites, to live on the positive side of the Yin Yang vs. the negative. Because both exist, doesn't mean we have to live in both of them. I believe we come to Planet Earth to learn how to transcend negativity, both within our selves and what we see in others and the world around us. We are meant to live in gratitude, thankfulness, love, understanding, compassion, non-judgment, and inner peace no matter what we see and what happens to us.

My lifetime has been a discipline to transform negative into positive, and the consequences of that is what you have experienced and mentioned. I was given a huge start on transforming negative feelings and thoughts while in Creative Initiative -- to look at my life and the people in it, and come to see that all was positive, forgiven, and with gratitude. This was done with great soul searching and emotion and just a lot of hard work. This can also be accomplished with intensive counseling by a good therapist who looks at cause vs. symptom. One can also do this on one's own, but it takes great motivation. The ability to investigate one's dark side is an opportunity few people have and the negative they feel can haunt them the rest of their life. If you feel there is <u>anything</u> in your past 40 years (starting with your earliest years), that you see as a negative, that is the place to start -- including injustices you have felt, things that made you mad or hurt, people that have let you down, things and people you blame. What that means is that you have not learned the lesson you were supposed to from that happening. When you glean the lesson, the negative thought and emotion will be transformed into a positive and you will be free of it.

In the last several years on my spiritual quest, I have encountered more teachers and more tools to transform what I might judge negative into something else. The reason I don't get upset when talking about something, or when something "bad" happens, is that I more likely view it as "just is." I don't label it bad so I am not angry that it happened. It is back to the "Resist not" of Jesus and "Stop the stopping" of Neale Donald Walsch. I do get caught up once in a while, but I don't stay there. I also believe that anger toward another is not justified, for the reasons above. It is one's own subjective reaction and is based in emotion, not fact.

Anger has never been my main emotion anyway; I tend to react with hurt feelings first. They go hand-in-hand and one must always look for the hurt behind the anger, because often it is what causes the anger. If hurt, look for the anger, and if angry, look for the hurt.

There is a discipline and a roadmap to move from negativity to positivity, and one has to want to do so. Few do. Most enjoy the drama and strength of the negative and feel justified in having it. A friend asked me recently what I loved; I was surprised at my own answer. Off the cuff, I said I loved the positive for its beauty and the negative for its strength. There is great power in the negative and it can be addictive. Only a few want to move to a higher ground. But the higher ground has the greatest treasures. I believe every experience we have is designed to move us to being a more positive person, to have more love for ourselves and others, to uncover our higher selves, to have inner peace, to find God within and in the world.

This movement out of the duality is the key to true freedom and inner peace, which most desire unconsciously. Most people think it is in outer things that brings these things -- status, money, a beautiful/strong physical body, youthfulness, the car, the "soul mate," the house, the job. The movement requires knowledge such as this and it involves practice and discipline. It involves looking at <u>why</u> something "makes you mad." Nothing really makes anyone mad. It is your decision to be mad; the instance is objective. It is the person who labels it "bad" and resists it.

My wish for you is to have inner peace and true freedom in your life. It is a journey. It is a discipline. It is a knowledge. It is the highest. It is our destiny.

Love,
Mom

ENDNOTES

Preface

1. The list of Universal Principles, which were the basis of this book, are Appendix A.

Introduction

1. Halliwell-Phillipps, J. O. *Nursery Rhymes and Nursery Tales of England:* Obtained Principally from the Oral Tradition. London: John Russell Smith, 1843. Print.

Chapter 2
Question #1: What Can I Reliably Base My Life On?

1. "What the Bleep Do We Know!?" *What the Bleep Do We Know!? & What the Bleep!? - Down the Rabbit Hole.* Web. 23 May 2010. <http://www.whatthebleep.com>.

2. Vitale, Joe, and Len Haleakala Hew. *Zero Limits: the Secret Hawaiian System for Wealth, Health, Peace, and More.* Hoboken, N.J.: Wiley, 2007. p. 63. Print.

3. Bhagavan Sri Sathya Sai Baba. "Heart2Heart, Divine Discourse of December 1, 1982." Message to the author. February 2008. E-mail.

4. *New Dimensions, Benefits Newsletter for UC Retirees* 26, #4 (Oct. 2009). Print.

5. "SEC Halts Internet-based Scam by Staten Island Firm Luring Investors with Phony Stock Tips and Fictional Trading Experts." *U.S. Securities and Exchange Commission.* United States Government, 20 Apr. 2010. Web. 21 May 2010. Its owner and four other employees were charged with

securities fraud and if convicted face up to 20 years in prison. <http://sec.gov/litigation/litreleases/2010/lr21494.htm>.

6. Theil, Stephen. "Is Capitalism Immoral?" *Deal Journal*. Wall Street Journal. 29 February 2008. Web. 31 Jan. 2009. <wsj.com>.

7. Preston, Robert. "Financial Crisis 'like a Tsunami' " *BBC*. 23 Oct. 2008. Web. 31 Jan. 2009. <news.bbc.co.uk/1/hi/business7687101.stm>.

8. Blanchard, Olivier. "World Growth 'worst for 60 Years' " *BBC*. 28 Jan. 2009. Web. 31 Jan. 2009. <news.bbc.co.uk/2/hi/business7856020.stm>.

9. Andrews, Edmund L. "Greenspan Concedes Error on Regulation." *New York Times* 23 Oct. 2008. Print.

10. Walsch, Neale Donald. *Tomorrow's God: Our Greatest Spiritual Challenge*. New York: Atria, 2004. p. 384. Print.

11. "Prayer of St. Francis of Assisi." (St. Francis 1181-1226) Web. 10 May 2010. < http://www.catholic-forum.com/saints/pray0027.htm>.

Chapter 3
Question #2: What do you do when evil gets in your house?

1. Dooley, Mike. "TUT...A Note from the Universe." Message to the author. E-mail. <http://www.tut.com/theclub/>.

2. Vitale, Joe, and Len Haleakala Hew. *Zero Limits: the Secret Hawaiian System for Wealth, Health, Peace, and More*. Hoboken, N.J.: Wiley, 2007. p. 62. Print.

3. *Abraham*, Channeled by Esther Hicks. Excerpt from the Workshop in Lincroft, N.J. October 15, 1996.

Chapter 4
How Do We Know What Is True?

1. Walsch, Neale Donald. *The New Revelations: a Conversation with God.* New York: Atria, 2002. p. 312. Print.

2. *The Bible.* Luke 6:48-49 Print.

3. Katie, Byron and Stephen Mitchell. *Loving What Is: Four Questions That Can Change Your Life.* New York: Harmony, 2002. p. 143. Print.

4. *Institute of Noetic Sciences: Home Page.* Web. 12 May 2010. <http://www.noetic.org/>.

5. Tiller, William A. *Welcome to the William A. Tiller Foundation.* Web. 11 May 2010.

6. Perhaps Translated or Written by Sir Richard Francis Burton.

7. Walsch, Neale Donald. *The New Revelations: a Conversation with God.* New York: Atria, 2002. p. 112. Print.

8. Walsch, Neale Donald

9. Walsch, Neale Donald. *Conversations with God: an Uncommon Dialogue.* Thorndike, Me.: G.K. Hall, 1997. pp. 51-52. Print.

Chapter 5
All Exists In Duality

1. Walsch, Neale Donald. "I Believe God Wants You to Know." Message to the author. 2 Oct. 2009. E-mail.

2. A Copy of the Letter Written in 1986 Is Appendix B.

3. Bhagavan Sri Sathya Sai Baba. "Heart2Heart, Divine Discourse of July 23, 2002." Message to the author. 30 June 2007. E-mail.

4. Tolle, Eckhart. *A New Earth: Awakening to Your Life's Purpose*. New York: Plume, 2006. 197. Print.

5. Walsch, Neale Donald. Walsch, Neale Donald. *Sharing a Law of Attraction Prosperity*. Neale Donald Walsch. Web. 11 May 2010. < http://prosperitytip.com/?p=54>.

6. Bhagavan Sri Sathya Sai Baba. "Heart2Heart, Divine Discourse of May 20,1993." Message to the author. 29 Feb. 2008. E-mail.

7. A Copy of the Letter, Written in 2009, Is Appendix C.

8. Walsch, Neale Donald. *Home with God: in a Life That Never Ends : a Wondrous Message of Love in a Final Conversation with God*. New York: Atria, 2006. 40. Print.

Chapter 6
All is One

1. Germain, David. "Oscar Buzz Surrounds Bullock, Bridges after Taking Home Statues; 'Hangover' Also Victorious." *Contra Costa Times* [Brentwood] 18 Jan. 2010, Morning Report ed., AA sec.: 1-2. Print.

2. Walsch, Neale Donald. *Tomorrow's God: Our Greatest Spiritual Challenge*. New York: Atria, 2004. Print.

3. Riley, Dorothy Winbush. *The Complete Kwanzaa: Celebrating Our Cultural Harvest*. New York: Castle, 2002. p. 9. Print.

4. Riley, Dorothy Winbush. *The Complete Kwanzaa: Celebrating Our Cultural Harvest*. New York: Castle, 2002. p. 34. Print.

5. Riley, D. Winbush. *The Complete Kwanzaa: Celebrating Our Cultural Harvest*. New York: Castle, 2002. pp. 34-35. Print.

6. Emoto, Masaru. *The Hidden Messages in Water*. New York: Atria, 2005. p. xxv. Print.

7. Ibid.

8. Emoto, Masaru. *The Hidden Messages in Water*. New York: Atria, 2005. p. 84. Print.

9. Weil, Simone. *Lectures on Philosophy*. Trans. Hugh Price. Cambridge UP, 1978. p. 214. Print.

10. Jackson, Michael. "Man in the Mirror." by Siedah Garrett. Rec. 1988. 1988. 14 Oct. 2006. Web. 11 May 2010. <http://www.youtube.com/watch?v=SgtWIx2zLtk>.

11. "We Are the Ones We Have Been Waiting For." *Wolf Lodge Cultural Foundation*. Web. http://www.wolflodge.org/hopi/hopi-old-oraibi.htm>.

12. Donne, John. *Devotions upon Emergent Occasions; Meditation SVII: Nunc Lento Sonitu Dicunt, Morieris*. Ann Arbor: University of Michigan, 1959. Print.

13. Lindelof, Bill. "Study: Woods' Woes Cost Shareholders $12 Billion." *Bay Area News Group (from Sacramento Bee)* [Brentwood] 29 Dec. 2009, Contra Costa Times ed., AA sec. Print.

14. Lao Tzu. "Quotations by Author." *The Quotations Page*. Web. 12 May 2010. <http://www.quotationspage.com/quotes/Lao-tzu/>.

15. *Great Integral Awakening Teleseminars - 14 Spiritual Luminaries Discuss Online Topics Such as Evolutionary Enlightenment, Spiral Dynamics, Transformative Spirituality and Evolution*. Web. 12 May 2010. <http://www.greatintegralawakening.com>.

16. Bhagavan Sri Sathya Sai Baba. "Heart2Heart, Divine Discourse of May 31, 1990." Message to the author. E-mail.

17. Walsch, Neale Donald. *Conversations with God: an Uncommon Dialogue*. Thorndike, Me.: G.K. Hall, 1997. p. 126. Print.

18. Bhagavan Sri Sathya Sai Baba. "Heart2Heart, Sai Inspires, Divine Discourse of October 13, 2002." Message to the author. 24 Aug. 2009. E-mail.

19. *Jo Dunning*. Web. 12 May 2010. <http://www.jodunning.com>.

20. Walsch, Neale Donald. *Conversations with God: an Uncommon Dialogue.* Thorndike, Me.: G.K. Hall, 1997. p. 52. Print.

21. Bahàu'llàh. (Founder of the Bahà'i Faith.) "Tablet to Mánikchí Sáhib -- 1.15." *Bahai Library Online*. Web. 12 May 2010.

22. Bhagavan Sri Sathya Sai Baba. "Bhagavan Sri Sathya Sai Baba." *My Space -- Groups.* International Sathya Sai Baba Organization, 4 July 1968. Web. 10 June 2008.

23. Kryon (spirit). *Welcome to the Kryon Website.* Web. 12 May 2010. <kryon.com>.

24. Bhagavan Sri Sathya Sai Baba. " 'Sai Inspires' Divine Discourse of May 21, 2000." Message to the author. 23 June 2007. E-mail.

25. Author Unknown, Possibly John Bradford, Australian Politician, Who While Imprisoned in the Tower of London, Saw a Criminal Going to Execution for His Crimes.

26. *The Bible*. Philippians 4:7. Print.

Chapter 7
We Are Spiritual Beings

1. Walsch, Neale Donald. *The New Revelations: a conversation with God.* New York: Atria Books. 2002. p. 2.

2. Bahaman Sri Sathya Sai Baba. Sai Inspires., Divine Discourse of December 30, 1977. 7/31/2009.

3. Walsch, Neale Donald. "The Little Soul and the Sun". *Conversations with God. Book 3 The Mind/Body Connection.* VT: Phoenix Books Inc. 2009. pp. 347-349.

4. Neale Donald Walsch. "I Believe God Wants you to Know." May 6, 2009. Internet email.

Chapter 8
The Unseen Controls the Seen

1. Kryon (spirit). "The Sacred Names and Functions of the Twelve Layers of DNA." *Kryon DNA Schedule.* Ed. Lee Carroll. Kryon/Lee Carroll. Web. MP3. 22 May 2010. <http://www.kryon.com/seminar%20images/DNA%20page/DNA.html>.

2. Veronica (spirit). Channeled by April Crawford. "Inner Whispers." Message to the author. January 6, 2010. E-mail.

3. Hall, Manly Palmer. *The Secret Teachings of All Ages.* VA: A&D Publishing. 2007, but originally written in 1928. p. 624.

4. Calleman, Dr. Carl J. and Mr. Ian Lungold "Why the Mayan Calendar?" <http://www.thewildrose.net/mayan_calendar_implications.html>.

5. 'Technology, Entertainment, Design -- Ideas Worth Spreading.' Profile on <http://www.TED.com>.

6. Ibid.

7. Taylor, Jill Bolte. *Stroke of Insight: a brain scientist's personal journey.* New York: Viking. 2008. p. 141.

8. Williamson, Marianne. *A Return To Love: Reflections on the Principles of A Course in Miracles.* New York: Harper Collins. 1992. p. 190-191.

9. Dr. Jayant's Blog. Internet, February 20, 2009.

10. Ryan, Glenn, Mike Atkinson and Rolan Macready. "The Physiological and Psychological Effects of Compassion and Anger." *Journal of Advancement in Medicine.* Summer (1995). Print.

11. Kryon, and Lee Carroll. "Quantum Healing." *Kryon Channelling.* Kryon/Lee Carroll. Web. MP3, Vancouver, BC.

26 January, 2008. <https://www.kryon.com/cartprodimages/downloadlvancouver_08.html>.

12. Bahaman Sri Sathya Sai Baba. "Heart2Heart, Sai Inspires, Divine Discourse of March 8, 1971." Message to the author. E-mail.

13. Allen, James. *As a Man Thinketh*. New York: Jeremy P. Tarcher/Penguin, 2006. p. 65. Print.

Chapter 9
Cause and Effect Always Occur Together

1. Emoto, Masaru. *The Hidden Messages in Water*. New York: Atria, 2005. p. 88. Print.

2. Kryon, and Lee Carroll. "Becoming even more quantum." *Kryon Channelling*. Kryon/Lee Carroll. Web. MP3, Pensacola, FL, January 30, 2010. <https://www.kryon.com/cartprodimages/download_pensacola_10.html>.

3. Klapper, Bradley Scott. "To the Skies, with Nary a Drop of Fuel." Bay Area News Group [Brentwood]. 8 April 2010, Morning Report. AA sec.: p. 4. Print.

Chapter 10
True Freedom is an Inner Attitude

1. "Warrior Quotes – the Teachings of Don Juan." Alignment 2012 – John Major Jenkins. Web. 19 May 2010. <http://alignment2012.com/warrior.html>.

Chapter 11
Change is a Constant

1. Diogenes, Laertius. *Lives of Eminent Philosophers*. Cambridge: Harvard UP, 2000. Print. Quoting Heraclitus.

2. Anonymous.

3. "Living Beating Cells Floor Exhibit." The Exploratorium. San Francisco, California. Exploratorium Digital Library.

4. Chopra, Deepak.

5. Tolle, Eckhart. *A New Earth: Awakening to Your Life's Purpose.* New York: Plume, 2006. Print.

6. The Light Party New Political Paradigm and Health Care. Web. 19 May 2010. <http://www.LightParty.com>.

7. Kaufman, Marc. (Washington Post) "A boost to the search for extraterrestrial life. Waiting for E.T.'s call is joint project for UC Berkeley, SETI Institute." *Bay Area News Group* [Brentwood 23 Dec. 2009, East County Times, California & the West ed., AA sec. p. 6. Print.

8. Powers, Ashley and DeeDee Correll (Los Angeles Times). "Measure would set protocol to give E.T. warm welcome. Voters being asked to approve welcoming panel for extraterrestrials." *Bay Area News Group* [Brentwood] 6 Dec. 2009, East County Times, California and the West ed., sec. A: p. 10. Print.

Chapter 12
After the Principles

1. "The Teachings of Abraham Law of Attraction." *Home of Abraham-Hicks Law of Attraction – It All Started Here!* Web. 19 May 2010. <http://www.abraham-hicks.com/teachings.php>.

2. Seth, channeled by Jane Roberts and Notes by Robert F. Butts. *Seth Speaks, The Eternal Validity of the Soul.* San Rafael, CA: New World Library, 1994. p. xv. Print.

Chapter 13
2012 and The Mayan Calendar

1. Braden, Gregg. "Choice Point 2012." *The Mystery of 2012. Preditions, Prophesies and Possibilities.* Boulder, CO: Sounds

True, 2009. P. 2. Print. Mr. Braden is an author and pioneer in bridging science and spirituality.

2. "Harmonic Convergence. August 17, 1987." *Harmonic Convergence – an Announcement of the Forthcoming End of Time*. The Wild Rose. Web. 15 June 2009. <http://www.thewildrose_net/harmonic_convergence>.

3. "Harmonic Convergence." Wikepedia.org. Web. 15 June 2009. <http://en.Wikepedia.org/wiki/Harmonic_Convergence>.

4. Ibid.

5. "Harmonic Convergence. August 17, 1987." *Harmonic Convergence – an Announcement of the Forthcoming End of Time*. The Wild Rose. Web. 15 June 2009. <http://www.thewildrose_net/harmonic_convergence>.

6. Ibid.

7. Piraro, Dan. "Bizarro (New)." Comic strip. Bay Area News Group [Brentwood] 21 Dec. 2009, Contra Costa Times ed. Print.

8. Browne, Sylvia, and Lindsay Harrison. *The End of Days: Predictions and Prophecies About the End of the World*. New York: Dutton, 2008. p. 3. Print. Ms. Browne is a spiritualist, Gnostic, psychic, and an author of many spiritual books.

9. Browne, Sylvia, and Lindsay Harrison. *The End of Days: Predictions and Prophecies About the End of the World*. New York: Dutton, 2008. pp. 3-10. Print.

10. Starbird. (Information from the High Council on Arcturus.). Message to the author. 9 Apr. 2010. E-mail <mws@stardoves.com>.

11. Calleman, Ph.D, Carl Johan. "2012: Mayan Wisdom 101." 2nd in a series. *Quantum Multimedia Productions with Dannion and Kathryn Brinkley*. http://www,QMPLV.com. 31 Mar. 2009. Web. 31 March 2009. Dr. Calleman has a doctorate in physical biology and has been studying the Mayan Calendar since 1979. He has written several books.

12. Russell, Peter, M.A., D.C.S. "A Singularity in Time". *The Mystery of 2012. Predictions, Prophesies and Possibilities.* Sounds True, 2009. pp. 24-29. Mr. Russell has degrees in theoretical physics, experimental psychology and computer science.

13. Russell, M.A., D.C.S., Peter. "A Singularity in Time." *The Mystery of 2012. Predictions, Prophesies and Possibilities.* Boulder, CO: Sounds True, 2009. Pp. 29-31. Print.

14. If you wonder if you are 'asleep,' 'half-awake,' or 'fully awake,' ask yourself: Who Am I? Your answer will tell you.

15. Kryon, and Lee Carroll. "Celebrate Gaia." *Kryon Channelling.* Kryon/Lee Carroll. Web. MP3, Mt. Shasta, CA, April 24, 2010. <https://www.kryon.com/cartprodimages/download_Shasta_10.html>.

16. Tolle, Eckhart. *A New Earth.* New York: Plume, 2006. Pp. 21-22. Print.

17. Braden, Gregg. "Choice Point 2012." *The Mystery of 2012. Preditions, Prophesies and Possibilities.* Boulder, CO: Sounds True, 2009. pp. 2-3. Print.

18. Arguelles, Ph.D., Jose'. "The Mayan Factor. Path Beyond Technology." *The Mystery of 2012. Predictions, Prophesies and Possibilities.* Boulder, CO: Sounds True, 2009. p. 7. Print.

Chapter 14
Calling All Evolutionaries

1. Koester, Jordan. "Religiosity. Is It Killing The Church. Prisoners From Within." *America's Good News* 6:10 (Oct. 2009). p. 1. Oakley, California.

2. Vallee, Martine (editor) with Lee Carroll & Kryon, Patricia Cori & The Sirian High Council, and Pepper Lewis & Gaia. *Transition Now. Redefining Duality 2012 And Beyond.* San Francisco, CA: Red Wheel/Weiser, LLC. p. 23. 2010. Print.

3. "Heaven On Earth / Lightworker Central." *Heaven On Earth / Home*. Web. 20 May 2010. <http://heavenly-light.us/lightworkers.htm>.

4. <http://www.onevoicemovement.org/>.

5. Anael. *Light and Love*. Bradfield. CD. This quote is taken from the booklet inside this CD. Web. <http:www.apsismusic.com>.

6. Yates, Shelley. Fire the Grid I: Be One. Web. 20 May 2010. <http:// www.FIRETHEGRID.com>.

7. Ibid.

8. Golman, Jonathan. Healing Sounds. Web. 10 Feb. 2010. <http://www.healingsounds.com>.

9. Calleman, Ph.D., Carl J., and Mr. Ian Lungold. "Why the Mayan Calendar?" Web. Aug. 2009. <http://thewildrose.net/mayan_calendar_implications.html>.

10. Walsch, Neale Donald. *Conversations With God, Book 2 Building The New Society*. Essex, VT: Phoenix, Inc., 2009. pp.175-176. Print.

11. "The Intender's Bridge." The Intenders of the Highest Good. Web. 20 May 2010 <http://www.intenders.com/>.

12. Hugo, Victor. (1802-1885)

www.ingramcontent.com/pod-product-compliance
Lightning Source LLC
Chambersburg PA
CBHW031246290426
44109CB00012B/454